Mark Ravenhill

Shoot / Get Treasure / Repeat

D0112524

Methuen Drama

Published by Methuen Drama 2008

1 3 5 7 9 10 8 6 4 2

Methuen Drama
A & C Black Publishers Limited
38 Soho Square
London W1D 3HB
www.acblack.com

ISBN: 978 1 408 10871 0

A CIP catalogue record for this book is available
from the British Library

Typeset by Country Setting, Kingsdown, Kent
Printed and bound in Great Britain by
Cox & Wyman Ltd, Reading, Berkshire

GATE National Theatre painesPLOUGH ROYAL COURT

3 – 20 April 2008

The Gate Theatre, the National Theatre, Out of Joint, Paines Plough, the Royal Court Theatre and BBC Radio 3 present

Mark Ravenhill's

SHOOT/GET

TREASURE/

REPEAT

An epic cycle of short plays

SHOOT/GET TREASURE/REPEAT was originally developed in association with the National Theatre Studio and Paines Plough, and was first produced as RAVENHILL FOR BREAKFAST at the Traverse Theatre, Edinburgh in August 2007 by Paines Plough, with the support of David Johnson.

www.shootgettreasurerepeat.com

MARK RAVENHILL

photo: Marc Brenner

Mark Ravenhill's first full-length play *Shopping and Fucking* was produced by Out Of Joint and the Royal Court Theatre in assocation with the NT Studio, and opened at the Ambassadors in 1996. His subsequent work includes *Faust is Dead* (Actors Touring Company), *Handbag* (ATC), *Some Explicit Polaroids* (Out Of Joint/West End), *Mother Clap's Molly House* (National Theatre/West End), *Totally Over You* (National Theatre/Shell Connections Festival), *Product* (Edinburgh Festival Fringe/ Paines Plough/Royal Court/European Tour), *The Cut* (Donmar Warehouse), *Citizenship* (National Theatre/Shell Connections) and *Pool (no water)* (Frantic Assembly/Lyric Hammersmith/Drum Theatre Plymouth). He also wrote the Barbican pantomime *Dick Whittington & His Cat* which opened in November 2006. Mark writes a regular culture comment column for The Guardian.

All Mark's plays are published by Methuen Drama Ltd and have been produced worldwide.

SHOOT/GET TREASURE/REPEAT

is an epic cycle of plays exploring the personal and political effect of war on modern life.

The plays that make up SHOOT/GET TREASURE/REPEAT began life at the 2007 Edinburgh Festival Fringe as *Ravenhill for Breakfast* (produced by Paines Plough), winning a Fringe First award, and the Jack Tinker Spirit of the Fringe award. They form a collage of very different scenes, with each taking its title from a classic work. Throughout April 2008, the plays are presented in various venues across London, from Notting Hill to a Victorian warehouse in Shoreditch, via Sloane Square and the South Bank.

Project Management by Schtanhaus

SCHTANHAUS

Special thanks to Guy Chapman, David Johnson and Adam Kenwright for their generous support of this production.

The Gate Theatre, the National Theatre, Out of Joint, Paines Plough, the Royal Court Theatre and BBC Radio 3 would also like to thank the following for their help with this production: All the actors and directors who took part in *Ravenhill for Breakfast*, Sarah Beckett, Toby Coffey, Auro and Jack Foxcroft, Rebecca Hanna-Grindall, Lisa Johnson, Mel Kenyon, Jemima Levick, George Perrin, Stephen Pidcock, Liz Smith, Robin Stephens, Charlotte Wilkinson.

Mark Ravenhill's

SHOOT/GET TREASURE/REPEAT

WOMEN OF TROY (triple bill with LOVE (BUT I WON'T DO THAT) and PARADISE LOST)
Paines Plough: Village Underground, dir. Roxana Silbert
Fri 18 Apr 6pm, Sat 19 Apr 11am, 2.30pm, 6pm, Sun 20 Apr 11am, 2.30pm
An American from the Midwest on TV: 'Why bomb us? We're the good guys.'

INTOLERANCE (double bill with CRIME AND PUNISHMENT)
National Theatre: Cottesloe
Fri 4 Apr 6pm, Sat 5 April 10am, 11am
A middle-class wife and mother suffers a repeated pain in her stomach.

WOMEN IN LOVE (double bill with ARMAGEDDON)
Gate Theatre, dir. Natalie Abrahami and Carrie Cracknell
Wed 16 – Fri 18 Apr 9.15pm
Dan is receiving treatment for cancer. Anna is loving, but maybe a bit too controlling.

FEAR AND MISERY (double bill with WAR AND PEACE)
Royal Court: Café Bar, dir. Dominic Cooke
Tue 15 Apr – Sat 19 Apr 8.45pm (Thur 11am)
An anxious couple plan their future while listening to the baby alarm.

WAR AND PEACE (double bill with FEAR AND MISERY)
Royal Court: Café Bar, dir. Dominic Cooke
Tue 15 Apr – Sat 19 Apr 9.45pm (Thur 12pm)
Alex, a seven-year-old child, is visited in his bedroom by a headless soldier.

YESTERDAY AN INCIDENT OCCURRED
BBC Radio 3, dir. Kate Rowland
Sun 20 April 8pm
Yesterday an unprovoked attack took place in the shopping centre. Why has no-one come forward
as a witness? Justice must be done if rights are to be matched with responsibilities.

Extracts from this production are available to hear at the Listening Point in the Royal Court Theatre (in the stairwell
on the first floor) for the duration of the cycle.

CRIME AND PUNISHMENT (double bill with INTOLERANCE)
National Theatre: Cottesloe
Fri 4 Apr 6pm, Sat 5 April 10am, 11am
A soldier interrogates a native woman in an occupied zone.

LOVE (BUT I WON'T DO THAT) (triple bill with WOMEN OF TROY and PARADISE LOST)
Paines Plough: Village Underground, dir. Roxana Silbert
Fri 18 Apr 6pm, Sat 19 Apr 11am, 2.30pm, 6pm, Sun 20 Apr 11am, 2.30pm
A soldier is embedded in a middle-class household in an occupied country. He is pushing for sex.

THE MIKADO (double bill with THE ODYSSEY)
National Theatre: Lyttelton
Thu 3 Apr 6pm, Sat 5 Apr 10am, 11am
Peter, who has cancer, expresses his anger to his partner.

WAR OF THE WORLDS (double bill with TWILIGHT OF THE GODS)
Paines Plough: Village Underground, dir. Roxana Silbert
Fri 18 Apr 7.30pm, Sat 19 Apr 12.30pm, 4pm, 7.30pm, Sun 20 Apr 12.30pm, 4pm
A chorus expresses grief for a city that has been bombed.

ARMAGEDDON (double bill with WOMEN IN LOVE)
Gate Theatre, dir. Natalie Abrahami and Carrie Cracknell
Wed 16 – Fri 18 Apr 9.15pm
Emma, a born-again Christian living in America's Bible Belt, arranges to meet a younger man.

THE MOTHER
Royal Court with Out of Joint: Jerwood Theatre Downstairs, dir. Max Stafford-Clark and Clare Lizzimore
Tue 8 Apr – Sat 12 Apr 6pm
Haley is visited by two soldiers who are going to break the news of her son's death in battle.

TWILIGHT OF THE GODS (double bill with WAR OF THE WORLDS)
Paines Plough: Village Underground, dir. Roxana Silbert
Fri 18 Apr 7.30pm, Sat 19 Apr 12.30pm, 4pm, 7.30pm, Sun 20 Apr 12.30pm, 4pm
Susan, whose country has been invaded, is being questioned by Jane.

PARADISE LOST (triple bill with WOMEN OF TROY and LOVE (BUT I WON'T DO THAT))
Paines Plough: Village Underground, dir. Roxana Silbert
Fri 18 Apr 6pm, Sat 19 Apr 11am, 2.30pm, 6pm, Sun 20 Apr 11am, 2.30pm
Liz decides to explore the screams coming from the flat below and discovers Ruth.

ODYSSEY (double bill with THE MIKADO)
National Theatre: Lyttelton, dir. Tom Cairns
Thu 3 Apr 6pm, Sat 5 Apr 10am, 11am
A group of soldiers prepare to go home after invading a foreign country.

BIRTH OF A NATION
Royal Court: Jerwood Theatre Downstairs, dir. Ramin Gray
Tue 8 Apr – Sat 12 Apr 9.30pm
A group of actors come to work with the local people after a foreign power has withdrawn.

PLATFORM DISCUSSION WITH MARK RAVENHILL
National Theatre: Cottesloe Theatre
Wed 9 Apr 6pm

(For venue information please refer to the pages that follow)

11 Pembridge Road, Notting Hill, London W11 3HQ

Box Office 020 7229 0706 Admin 020 7229 5387 Fax 020 7221 6055 www.gatetheatre.co.uk

"One of the major generators of theatrical talent in this country" Stephen Daldry

The Gate Theatre in Notting Hill occupies a unique place in London and British theatre and has done for nearly thirty years. The Gate is a small, ambitious theatre known for its inventive use of space and the exceptional artists it attracts.

An environment in which artists can create first-class and original theatre, the Gate is a springboard that allows emerging artists to excel and make their mark. With an audience capacity of between fifty and seventy people, the space has challenged and inspired directors and designers, making it famous for being one of the most flexible and transformable spaces in London.

"One of the thrills of a Gate production is the endless inventiveness applied to a tiny space: you never know what will greet you as you walk through the door." The Metro

The Gate relies on artistic dedication and the generous support of individuals. Never deterred by financial limitations, the Gate continues to break boundaries and present the very best in world theatre. For more information on the Gate's work, please visit www.gatetheatre.co.uk.

Artistic Directors **Natalie Abrahami** and **Carrie Cracknell**
Producer **Jo Danvers**
General Manager **Undine Engelmann**
Technical Manager **Nick Abbott**
Education Manager **Lynne Gagliano**

National Theatre, South Bank, London SE1 9PX

Tel: 020 7452 3000 Fax: 020 7452 3030 info@nationaltheatre.org.uk www.nationaltheatre.org.uk

The National Theatre is central to the creative life of the UK. In its three theatres on the South Bank in London it presents an eclectic mix of new plays and classics from the world repertoire, with seven or eight productions in repertory at any one time. And through an extensive programme of amplifying activities – Platform performances, backstage tours, foyer music, publications, exhibitions and outdoor events – it recognises that theatre doesn't begin and end with the rise and fall of the curtain.

The National also has a Studio, providing an environment where writers, actors and practitioners of all kinds can explore, experiment, and devise new work, free from the pressure of public performance.

National Theatre Director **Nicholas Hytner**
Executive Director **Nick Starr**
Finance Director **Lisa Burger**
Literary Associate Director **Sebastian Born**
Marketing Director **Sarah Hunt**

For SHOOT/GET TREASURE/ REPEAT
Producer **Angus MacKechnie,** with **Sarah Mowat** and **Emily Thomas**

out of joint

7 Thane Works, Thane Villas, London N7 7NU

Tel: 020 7609 0207 Fax: 020 7609 0203 ojo@outofjoint.co.uk www.outofjoint.co.uk

"You expect something special from Out of Joint" The Times

Out of Joint is a national and international touring theatre company dedicated to the development and production of new writing. Under the direction of Max Stafford-Clark the company has premiered plays from leading writers including David Hare, Caryl Churchill, Alistair Beaton, Sebastian Barry and Timberlake Wertenbaker, as well as introducing first-time writers such as Simon Bennett, Stella Feehily and Mark Ravenhill.

"Max Stafford-Clark's excellent Out of Joint company" The Independent

Touring all over the UK, Out of Joint frequently performs at and co-produces with key venues such as the Royal Court and the National Theatre. The company has performed in six continents – most recently a world tour of its Africa-inspired *Macbeth*. Back home, Out of Joint also pursues an extensive education programme.

"Out of Joint is out of this world" Boston Globe

Out of Joint's next project is a co-production with Sydney Theatre Company, *The Convict's Opera* – an adaptation of John Gay's *The Beggar's Opera* – by Stephen Jeffreys.

Director **Max Stafford-Clark**
Producer **Graham Cowley**
Marketing Manager **Jon Bradfield**
Administrator & Education Manager **Rebecca Pilbeam**
Assistant Director **Clare Lizzimore**
Literary Manager **Alex Roberts**
Finance Officer **Sandra Palumbo**
PA & Office Assistant **Maeve McKeown**

Board of Directors Kate Ashfield, Linda Bassett, John Blackmore (Chair), Elyse Dodgson, Sonia Friedman, Stephen Jeffreys, Paul Jesson, Danny Sapani, Karl Sydow.

To buy copies of playtexts like this by writers such as Mark Ravenhill and many more, visit www.outofjoint.co.uk.

painesPLOUGH   Fri 18 – Sun 20 April

Fourth Floor, 43 Aldwych, London, WC2B 4DN

Tel: 020 7240 4533 Fax: 020 7240 4534 office@painesplough.com www.painesplough.com

Paines Plough is an award-winning, nationally and internationally renowned theatre company, specialising exclusively in commissioning and producing new plays.

"The ever-inventive Paines Plough" The Independent

Inspired by the creativity of its writers and collaborators Paines Plough has embraced the challenge of diversifying the way in which it works. Paines Plough's national footprint is far-reaching; the company's work has recently been seen late at night in the depths of London's West End; over lunch on the South Bank; in St. Petersburg and Bradford, New York and Plymouth; on the Globe Stage and in a cupboard in Brighton.

Paines Plough seeks out partners with whom it can collaborate in a bold, responsive spirit to generate truly contemporary theatre.

Artistic Director **Roxana Silbert**
General Manager **Ushi Bagga**
Literary Manager **Pippa Ellis**
Interim Administrative Assistant **Fiona Gregory**
Playwright in Residence **Tom Morton-Smith**
(supported by The Fenton Arts Trust and Arts Council England)
Pearson Playwright **Duncan MacMillian**
Press Representation **Sheridan Humphries** (07966 578607)

To find out more and join the Paines Plough mailing list visit www.painesplough.com
Paines Plough is a Registered Charity No 26752

Paines Plough will be presenting their plays from SHOOT/GET TREASURE/REPEAT at Village Underground, 54 Holywell Lane, London EC2A 3PQ.

Village Underground is a new cultural space in the heart of Shoreditch. An amalgamation of two intrinsic elements – a collection of ex London Underground tube train carriages recycled to form creative studios, coupled with the voluminous raw space of its restored Victorian warehouse, transformed into a flexible and multifunctional arena.

Village Underground is socially driven, a charitable organisation and environmentally conscious. Commercial uses directly support the production of new creative work and emerging cultural practitioners. This essential balance allows us to act as a stage – facilitating a vibrant and diverse cross section of creative endeavour, cultural hybrid and artistic collaboration.

For more information visit www.villageunderground.co.uk

Sloane Square, London, SW1W 8AS

Tel: 020 7565 5000 Fax: 020 7565 5001 info@royalcourttheatre.com www.royalcourttheatre.com

"For me the theatre is really a religion or way of life. You must decide what you feel the world is about and what you want to say about it, so that everything in the theatre you work in is saying the same thing ... A theatre must have a recognisable attitude. It will have one, whether you like it or not."
George Devine, first artistic director of the English Stage Company: notes for an unwritten book.

As Britain's leading national company dedicated to new work, the Royal Court Theatre produces new plays of the highest quality, working with writers from all backgrounds, and addressing the problems and possibilities of our time.

"The Royal Court has been at the centre of British cultural life for the past 50 years, an engine room for new writing and constantly transforming the theatrical culture." Stephen Daldry

Since its foundation in 1956, the Royal Court has presented premieres by almost every leading contemporary British playwright, from John Osborne's *Look Back in Anger* to Caryl Churchill's *A Number* and Tom Stoppard's *Rock 'n' Roll*. Just some of the other writers to have chosen the Royal Court to premiere their work include Edward Albee, John Arden, Samuel Beckett, Edward Bond, Jez Butterworth, Martin Crimp, Ariel Dorfman, Christopher Hampton, David Hare, Eugène Ionesco, Ann Jellicoe, Terry Johnson, Sarah Kane, David Mamet, Martin McDonagh, Conor McPherson, Mark Ravenhill, Wole Soyinka, Polly Stenham, David Storey, debbie tucker green, Arnold Wesker and Roy Williams.

"It is risky to miss a production there" Financial Times

In addition to its full-scale productions, the Royal Court also facilitates international work at a grass roots level, developing exchanges which bring young writers to Britain and sending British writers, actors and directors to work with artists around the world. The Royal Court Young Writers' Programme also works to develop new voices with their bi-annual Festival and year-round development work for writers under the age of 26.

"Yes, the Royal Court is on a roll. Yes, Dominic Cooke has just the genius and kick that this venue needs... It's fist-bitingly exciting." Independent

Artistic Director **Dominic Cooke**
Executive Director **Kate Horton**
Associate Producer **Diane Borger**
Casting Director **Amy Ball**
Production Managers **Sue Bird, Paul Handley**

BBC Radio 3, Broadcasting House, London, W1A 1AA

www.bbc.co.uk/radio3

BBC Radio 3 makes available a broad spectrum of classical music, jazz, world music, drama and arts discussions. The network focuses on presenting live and specially recorded music of the highest quality from the UK and beyond, including a variety of contributions from the BBC's own performing groups. Radio 3 plays a role in shaping the national cultural agenda through its promotion of musical performance; its commissioning of music, and through its ideas and drama programmes including *The Wire* and *The Sunday Play*.

Controller **Roger Wright**
Head of Speech Programmes **Abigail Appleton**

BBC Writersroom, Grafton House, 379-381 Euston Road, London NW1 3AU

www.bbc.co.uk/writersroom

BBC writersroom identifies and champions new writing talent and diversity across BBC drama, comedy and children's programmes through a range of targeted development schemes. Writersroom manages the unsolicited script system across the BBC, where writers of any experience can send in original scripts as a calling card of their talent. They invest in new writing projects nationwide and build creative partnerships, including work with theatres, writers' organisations and film agencies across the country.

Creative Director, New Writing **Kate Rowland**

SCHTANHAUS   Project Manager

4th Floor, 43 Aldwych, London, WC2B 4DN

Tel: 020 7240 4087 Fax: 0844 870 0267 mail@schtanhaus.co.uk www.schtanhaus.co.uk

Schtanhaus is a producing engine, founded in 2004 by Tom Morris and Emma Stenning. As well as producing work for established companies such as Filter Theatre (*Faster, Body Stories, Twelfth Night, Water*), the RSC (Filter's *Twelfth Night* and A&BC's *Henry VIII* both for Complete Works Festival) or Paines Plough (Mark Ravenhill's SHOOT/GET TREASURE/REPEAT), Schtanhaus has also launched Carl Heap's company beggarsbelief (producing *World Cup Final, Jason and the Argonauts* and *St George and the Dragon*, commissioning *Gunfight At The OK Corral* and developing *Tombstone Tales*) and this year sees the launch of Theatre of the Unexpected, a vehicle for surprising work led by Tom Morris.

Schtanhaus also pursues a number of independent projects, and over the past two years has produced *Oogly Boogly*, Guy Dartnell and Tom Morris's improvised performance piece for 12-18 month old babies and Tim Barlow's *Earful*.

Future projects for the company includes Filter's *Twelfth Night* on national and international tour, beggarsbelief's *Tombstone Tales* on national tour, Theatre of the Unexpected research and development on Rory Stewart's *Occupational Hazards*, Beethoven's *Opus 131*, and *Romeo and Juliet*. Schtanhaus is also working with Helen Chadwick, Hampton Court Palace and Simon Godwin.

Directors **Emma Stenning** and **Tom Morris**
Producing Team **Sally Gibson, Jo Evans, Lydia Spry** and **Ric Watts**
Financial Director **Daniel Morgenstern**

For SHOOT/GET TREASURE/REPEAT
Project Management **Jo Evans**

Shoot / Get Treasure / Repeat

Contents

Introduction

Shoot / Get Treasure / Repeat is an epic cycle of short plays. I was
driven to write like this because I spotted two contradictory
needs in contemporary audiences. We still have that urge for
an epic narrative that draws us to the *Oresteia* or *Paradise Lost* or
Shakespeare's history plays. But also we are the children of the
sound-bite age, able to absorb information and narrative in a
few quick seconds from the various screens that surround us.
We have a soundtrack to our lives on a constant shuffle on our
iPods. We want the mega and we want the micro, the super-
size-me and the sushi – all at the same time.

So, in exploring our contemporary urge to bring our own values
and definitions of freedom and democracy to the whole planet,
I've chosen to suggest a big picture through little fragments.
I've named each of the fragments after an existing epic.

It's up to you in which sequence you read or stage the plays:
they are presented in this volume in the order they were written
and that order has a certain logic. But you might choose to
'shuffle' the plays into a different order and see what that offers
you. You might just cherry-pick the ones that seem most relevant
to you. Hopefully different readers, theatres and audiences
will experiment with different combinations and so different
experiences will emerge. I think this reflects the age we live in,
an age in which we yearn for a grand narrative even as we
suspect it is dead.

As you can see by flicking through the book, some of the plays
have fixed character names and locations, others offer more
fluid possibilities for the number of actors used and the setting
of the play. Where no characters are named, the indent like
this (–) is a suggestion, but not a strict rule, that another actor
speaks. See what works for you. Someimes I also use this (/)
which means the next actor starts talking, creating an overlap.

I was supported and encouraged by many people in the marathon
task of putting these plays together but nobody more so than
Roxanna Silbert. She's a marvel. So, to Rox – respect, babe.

Mark Ravenhill, April 2008

Play One

Women of Troy

A chorus of **Women.**

–   We want to ask you this. I want to ask you: why do you bomb us?

–   We all . . . All of us: why do you bomb us?

–   Yes. Why . . . ?

–   Just . . . tell us – why?

–   You see. We are the good people. Just look at us. Take a look at us. Take a good look at all of us. Gathered here today. And what do you see? You see the good people.

–   I don't get . . . I can't see . . . why would you bomb the good people?

–   Can I talk about me? I'd like to talk about me. Every morning I wake up, I take my fruit and I put it in the blender and I make smoothies for my family. My good family. My good partner and my good child. For Thomas and for Zachary. And yet you –

–   And me. Every morning I sit down with my good mother, with Marion, and we eat bacon and eggs and pancakes. A good meal. And yet you –

–   Me. Every morning I read the paper. I read about the . . . There is suffering in the world. There is injustice. Food is short. This morning a soldier was killed. His head blown off. I am moved about that. I care. As any good person would. And yet you –

–   My husband likes to be out early washing the SUV. Every morning washing the . . . which is . . . he washes the SUV every morning. Maybe . . . But still, it's a good car. We live in a good place. It's a good community. All of our neighbours are

good people. Here, behind the gates, we are good people. The
people you –

–   I only eat good food. Ethical food. Because I believe that
good choices should be made when you're shopping. All of my
choices are good choices. They really are. So don't you –

–   'A good breakfast sets you up for the day,' my father always
said. 'You have a good meal at the start of the day.' And he
had bacon and black pudding and sausages and sometimes a
burger and . . . for every day of his sixty-four years. He was a
good man. I miss him so much. My partner understands. And
now you –

–   I work for the good of our society. Every day I deal with
the homeless and the addicted and the mad and the lost. They
come to me and I try to do what I can for them. I try to mend
their broken wings. I use the arts to heal them. Drama or
dance or painting. We'll . . . well, we'll . . . like we put on a
little play. They all heal. Which is . . . that is a good thing to
do. I'm doing good while you're . . . Do you see who am I?
Do you? Do you see how good I am? As we all are good. How
good we all are. How good freedom and democracy truly is.
So please don't hurt . . .

–   That is wrong. Wrong. Why are you doing this?

–   Why?

–   We are the – no doubt about that – good people.

–   That's right, the good people. The good guys. The righteous
ones.

–   You're just blowing us up like this –

–   It's frightening. It's horrific. It's horrible.

–   Blowing us up. My friend, an old dear friend from the
university, she, oh . . .

–   Come on, hey hey hey, you don't have to, you don't have
to –

–   She was such a good person. She was a truly good person.

−   No no, calm yourself, no −

−   I want to, okay? I want to speak out, okay? Okay? Okay? Okay?

−   Okay.

−   Because you understand what good men and good people and good children you are destroying, our civilisation, a world of good people.

−   Yes.

−   My friend from the university was on the bus that morning. She was going to the department of political science. And that fucking − oh sorry − those flames just tore through her body and she was thrown through the window and she lay there screaming on the pavement. She was an angel. That woman, all her life an angel and now she's lying there screaming, calling out in pain, 'HELP OH HELP OH HELP OH HELP − '

−   Come on, you don't −

−   I want to −

−   This isn't good for you −

−   No, they have to see, they have to see the good people, they . . . She was an angel. She was a rock. She . . . she died in the hospital an hour later of her injuries. And what had she ever done in her life but good?

−   Our way of life is the right, the good, it's the right life.

−   It's the only way of life −

−   The only way of life. Freedom, Democracy, Truth − so why? Please why?

−   Why do you bomb us?

−   Please, we want to understand. We want to. Why do you bomb . . . ?

−   I remember when I heard about the bombings, about the wave of destruction, I was . . . I was . . . juicing. Thomas was in the shower, Zachary was watching a DVD. And suddenly flames were engulfing our world. Members of my civilisation were burning up and screaming and dying in pain. I felt what they felt. It was awful and I just sat there and I thought I just honestly thought I sat there and I thought: why would anyone do this to the good people?

–   I took Alex to the school in the SUV. We drove through the gates of our community in the SUV and the news of the bombings came through on the car radio. They stopped the music and they told us about the bombs that were . . . everywhere. Alex began to cry. I mean, what do you do? What do you do? He was seven. I turned off the radio but he screamed out to me: 'Mummy, Mummy, what's happening? Why are they doing this? Aren't we good people?' And I said, 'Of course we are, darling, of course we are, we are very good people.'

–   Good for you.

–   Good for you.

–   Good for you.

–   We know your culture's very different.

–   And that's okay. We accept that.

–   We tolerate, we accept, we celebrate –

–   We celebrate – exactly – we celebrate difference.

–   It's all part of being a good people.

–   It's what makes us the good people that we are.

–   Everywhere. Good good good good good good good good good good good good people. Please, you're good. Of course you are. You must be . . . Please, show me a little good.

–   I want to imagine you . . . Help me. Help me imagine you –

–   I want to imagine you going to the garden centre. I want to imagine you taking your son and your husband in the SUV and choosing a – I don't know – a bench. A garden bench. I want to picture that. Just to see you as . . . normal. But somehow . . .

– I want to see you: it's night, it's three in the morning, maybe your lover is ill and you reach out to him in the night, your fingers brush his fingers, you touch him and you say 'I love you' and he says 'I love you' back and there's a little ripple of fear through you – does he mean it? – before he reaches out and holds you through the night. I really want to, I want to see you . . . this is what we do . . . this is what the good people do. But are you doing it? I can't see that. I want to see that. But I – oh I can't see that –

– Of course we've had enemies before, of course we've fought wars, but I still . . . still . . . I saw the old enemies drinking coffee, their . . . eating their breakfast . . . I could picture that . . . I could picture them . . . They had breakfast, babies, they made love . . . but you . . .

– Look at me. Look at me. Don't be so strange – just look at me.

– Oh.

– Oh.

– I see nothing when I look at you.

– I see . . . darkness. I see –

– Everything that is . . . you are opposite and – oh shit, this is hard . . .

– You are so different.

– ATTENTION. THERE'S A CAR. THERE'S A CAR PARKED RIGHT OUTSIDE THE HOSPITAL AND IT'S PACKED WITH EXPLOSIVES AND IT'S WAITING TO DRIVE ITS WAY INTO THE HOSPITAL.

– Again?

– This is too much.

– On and on and on and on and on.

– A HOSPITAL WARD HAS JUST BEEN BOMBED. A MAN CARRYING A BACKPACK WALKED ONTO

A HOSPITAL WARD. IT IS BELIEVED THAT THE
BACKPACK CONTAINED HIGH EXPLOSIVES. SEVEN
PATIENTS AND STAFF DIED IMMEDIATELY IN THE
BLAST, ANOTHER TWENTY SUFFERED SEVERE
BURNS. THE AUTHORITIES HAVE CORDONED OFF
A LARGE SECTION OF THE NEW TOWN.

– Oh my God.

– Oh shit oh shit oh shit.

– Why have you bombed us? You bastards.

– Why have you bombed us?

– Why have you bombed all those good people? It's just . . .
I can't begin to . . .

– There were people in there, you bastards, people with cancers
and strokes and heart attacks and Aids and dementias and you
have – you have bombed those good people –

   Nurses. Is there a better person than a nurse? I don't think
so. I don't think . . . I think a Nurse is the goodest, the best
per-per-per-per, the people, nurses are the best, best good
people, the people, the people, the people, the people who do
the best good, the, the, the the the the the total . . . they do
more good . . . they do good . . . in this whole wide world and
you have blown them apart and you have torn them apart and
you have consumed their bodies in flames. You cunts, you
cunts, you cunts, you utter, you – yeah.

– Look, I'm going to be honest, okay, I'm going to be totally
totally honest, okay?

– Do it.

– Just do it just do it just do it just do it just do it.

– You are not a person. I don't see you as a person. I've never
seen you as a person. You're a bomb. I look at you. And all
I see is a bomb. I see you there now and I see you and I hear
you ticking away and I feel frightened and angry and disgusted.
That's what I feel.

– I want to forgive you. Is it too late? You've bombed all those . . . Is it too late to forgive . . . Do you understand the idea, the word, I FORGIVE? A nurse burning up. I see it in my . . .

– I want to – okay – I want to . . . We can trade with you, okay? There's natural resources, okay, and let's take the natural resources and let's take the natural resources and let's yes . . . what do you . . . A nurse burning up . . . what do you say, huh?

– Look at you. Tick tick tick tick tick tick. That's all you – you monster – that's all you –

– And there's the multimedia environment, would you like that, bet you would. Come on, yeah? The multimedia environment that would be oooh – freedom democracy democracy freedom the multimedia environment nurse flames – that would be good fun. What d'ya say?

– You EVIL EVIL EVIL EVIL EVIL –

– And shopping. I can give you as many . . . I can bring you as many . . . you really can, I promise you, you can have as many – flames nurse – you can have shops and I have travelled this world up and down and down and up and round and I have not discovered a woman or a man, a man or a woman who does not – nurse nurse nurse – love to shop.

– Democracy and freedom. Freedom and democracy. I offer them to you. I'm giving them to you. Don't be frightened. Don't be alarmed. Do they seem – nurse in flames – like big difficult words? Well, they're not, they're not, they're –

– Instincts.

– Exactly, they are – good, they are human instincts and if you'll just – we can liberate you and then you'll understand, you'll embrace, you'll live, you'll enjoy freedom and democracy. Think of that you'll have freedom and democracy.

– (*Punches air.*) Hurrah!

– (*Punches air.*) Hurrah!

– (*Punches air.*) Hurrah!

– You can be good people, good persons, good you can you –

– PLEASE LISTEN CAREFULLY. YOU ARE ABOUT TO DIE. WE HAVE INFILTRATED THIS SITE. A SUICIDE BOMBER IS INSIDE YOUR SITE AND YOU ARE ABOUT TO DIE. MESSAGE ENDS.

– No! No! No! I'm a good person.

– Me too. I'm good. I'm good. I'm good.

– Lord protect us Lord protect us Lord protect us.

– I love you, Tom. I love you, Zachary. Zac – your paintings on the fridge that I'm so proud of. I love them. Thomas – our evenings of fish and wine and colleagues from the university. Good evenings. You are a good man. I love you.

– Marion, you are a good mother. Our breakfasts mean so much to me. Our good breakfasts where we talk about the good day that lies ahead. Marion, Mother, I love you.

– Please. Go to the garden bench. Go the garden bench and sit on the garden bench and think of that day at the garden centre. Such an ordinary day but still a good day, wasn't it? Wasn't it? Wasn't it a good day? It was. I love you.

– Please don't have too much coffee. Please don't have too much sugar. Please don't – no do, do, do . . . Oh you always were such a good flirt. I love you.

– Come on, pull the, squeeze the trigger, push the button. We're ready.

– We're ready now to go. Ready and – at peace, loved. Are you?

– Ready and we are oh so sure so sure so sure – we are the good people the good people.

– The good people.

– The good people.

–   And the Lord made His earth for us, His earth with its resources and its . . . coffee, the bombs, the shops . . . they are for us. For us to use the good people. And we will use them, we will.

–   We stand together now.

–   We stand together stand strong.

–   We are ready for death.

–   Which of you is the suicide bomber? Identify yourself. Come forward. Come forward.

A **Man** *steps from the crowd with a backpack on.*

Man   I am the suicide bomber.

–   You can kill us, detonate your . . . blow our bodies apart, rip our heads from our . . . consume us in your flames because we will die a good death.

–   A good death for a good people.

–   A good death for a good people.

–   Hallelujah!

–   Hallelujah!

–   Hallelujah!

–   But if there's good people, don't you see that? If there's good there's got to be there must be – you see?

–   Yes.

–   Bad people. Can't have good without bad. Bad without good. I never thought before. But now I'm . . .

–   The flames burning up all our angels.

–   Maybe you are bad people, yes?

–   Well, maybe that's right, huh? Maybe that's right? Maybe we are the good people and you are the evil, wicked, terrible – maybe you are the bad people.

–   Yes yes yes. Bad people, And maybe eventually the time has come when there's good and bad and the great battle will begin.

–   The never-ending battle of good and evil.

–   And maybe we've been pretending, maybe we've been dreaming, maybe we've been numbing ourselves.

–   Maybe this is the truth about us. And maybe this is the truth about you. Maybe you are evil.

–   I'm sorry to say that. We're sorry to say that. We look at you and we . . .

–   This is the end for us, this is the . . . But this is just the beginning of the war. The good people . . . there's an army of the good people and they're standing up now and they are fighting you and this is a war that is going to go on forever.

–   Forever.

–   For good. For us this is the end, but for the war it is just the beginning.

–   The war begins.

–   Here.

–   Now.

–   Today.

–   You tear our bodies apart so the great war between good and evil can begin.

–   The beginning. Amen.

Man   Paradise!

Bomb blast. The **Man** *and the* **Women** *die. A great white light that blinds the spectators. Out of it steps a* **Soldier**, *half-man, half-angel.*

Soldier   I have been sleeping. But now I wake. For centuries I roamed the planet and created this world. But then I saw what I had made and I slept. My job was done. But I was wrong. My job was not done.

Freedom and democracy and truth and light – the fight is never done. There are always enemies. We must fight.

He kisses the lips of each of the dead **Women** *in turn.*

Soldier   I promise you that gun and tank and this flaming sword will roam the globe until everywhere is filled with the goodness of the good people.

There will be good everywhere.

And then, every day, peace will be war. Keeping the peace with the gun. It is my destiny.

I open battle.

I declare war.

Begin.

He lifts his sword high and a great army fills the stage.

Kill the bombers. Slaughter our enemies. In the name of the good people – begin.

Play Two

Intolerance

Middle-class kitchen. Breakfast time. **Helen** *sits with a smoothie, a probiotic yogurt and the post. Off, the sound of a DVD of a children's animation.*

Helen   This is a mixture of raspberries and cranberries and apple juice.

I used to – there was a lot of caffeine in my gut. And I used to hurt. I really –

Sometimes I would be doubled up with – I would be – I would try to talk to you –

For instance, I might be trying to talk to you – just to tell you that you're lovely or special or –

And suddenly I would shoot with pain.

And I would stop

I would just stop talking to you.

And sort of –

And I became worried that I was holding in an agony, a –

Oh I don't know, a –

And I ran over and over my life and I realised –

No.

Everything is perfect.

My life has been . . .

A happy family. Grass and swingball and mountains and barbecues.

School was happy. No pressure to learn.

University. I passed. Nothing special but then I'm not . . .

And I met Thomas.

He ticked the boxes that I ticked on the form and a year later we were buying together.

This apartment is lovely.

I once – only once – had an argument with the woman downstairs – but she is now in rehab and it's quiet as the top of a mountain in this apartment.

There's a little more berry than juice in this this morning.

Which in my book is a good thing.

Your very good health!

She drinks the smoothie.

Breakfast. Quiet.

I don't read the newspapers or watch the news or anything.

There's bombs and wars and . . .

They only upset you really and what can you do?

If I'm going to be blown up – so be it.

As long as I'm in the centre of the blast.

Breakfast is my favourite time of the day. My time.

Thomas is in the shower.

Zachary is watching a DVD in his bedroom before school.

And I'm here – with my juice.

I remember the day that I discovered the key. My intolerance.

I felt foolish.

Foolish because I thought my pain must have run deep.

In one session with the – what was the name of that woman who regressed me?

Oh it goes, it goes. Her name has . . .

Anyway, one day she takes me so far back.

I'm with the angels. I am an – I don't even have the words . . .

There was no religion in my school or family or town so –

I am an – I suppose – an archangel. But with Lucifer I am banished.

And I'm supposed to fall into Hell with the rebel army. But I don't.

For some reason –

The whole army – one half of Heaven – is sucked into Hell. And throughout the cosmos you can hear their screams.

They're still screaming to this day. It's just –

It's just –

But for whatever, for whatever, I don't know why –

My fall is disturbed, it doesn't go quite right.

And so I end up in Eden on my own.

I mean in Eden with my wing hanging loose and hurting beside me.

But there's nuts and berries.

But I'm so alone.

No God, no Lucifer – nobody.

I try to tell stories. But stories in Eden for yourself. For eternity.

It's pretty fucking pointless.

Hello! Hello! My wing has broken –

There was once a man who lived by a –

No no no.

The man runs towards her, in his hand the missing –

No no no no.

Fucking pointless.

What's the fucking point?

Day after perfect day on my own with my wing hanging by my side.

So one day I hang myself from a tree.

Ha. Heh. Heh. That seems so silly now.

But at the time when you're being regressed –

I suppose that woman –

Inga! That was it! Inga! She was called Inga!

I had to take antihistamines because of the cats.

I suppose Inga was a charlatan.

Because that woman discovered that I had fifteen previous lives. I lived them all.

But still a year later I was doubling up with pain.

I flew once to a client. I'd flown three hours, she'd flown five. It was her only window that year.

And for the whole weekend I just lay on the bed in the hotel room screaming with the agony.

She'd call up from the lobby every now and then and it took all I had just to push my lips into the right shape for –

Sorry, still in too much pain.

And she'd say –

Not to worry. I can go shopping.

That poor woman.

This place was – I mean it was one of those places where they'd only had civilisation –

It was the first few years.

So the shopping was extremely poor.

God, she must have been miserable.

And by the time I recovered she'd had to go back.

Her little boy's mood swings had kicked in again. His medication needed playing with.

I had wasted both our time.

Acupuncture would take it away for a few days.

Then the pain would be back.

Then I developed a phobia of the needles.

Thomas was so loving through all of this. Thomas is such a wonderful man.

He would anticipate the pain.

He could see it coming in my face and he'd whisk Zachary away and sit him in front of a DVD.

I'm very lucky to have Thomas

He'll be out of the shower soon.

He teaches political science in the university and travels widely because he thinks in an original way and there's a market for that.

If you have an original idea you can set your price very high.

That's what Thomas tells his students. I don't know whether they listen. But they'll learn.

Some of them come back to him a couple of years after graduation and say –

I've learnt how to sell myself.

And we raise a glass of white wine to them that evening over supper.

Here's to another one finally learning that Thomas is a very wise man.

It takes a few years but they get there in the end.

This is a probiotic yogurt.

The main thing is no caffeine, but I think this plays its part in keeping the pain away.

It makes sense. Active culture in your gut helps to keep you happy.

She eats the yogurt.

I tried acupressure when I got too scared of the needles but it didn't do anything for me. But it seemed to have no effect.

And I became resigned. I said to Thomas: I will be living the rest of my life in pain.

And he said: no no no no.

I suppose therapy in the conventional sense is pretty much . . . over.

I don't understand, but at supper parties in our new apartment when Thomas's colleagues from the faculty would come and I would give them fish that was the consensus.

But I was in pain. Every day. Sometimes for several hours.

Sometimes I wasn't seeing Zachary. We weren't snuggling up together in front of a DVD like a mother and child should do.

For a while I believed that therapist.

Actually, you know, actually a very long time.

When I think, if the time and the money –

I am an unashamedly classic analyst, he told me. So I nodded and there was a couch and it was several years and I went very early and we would –

I mean this was before breakfast. This was very early.

I'd get in the car and cross the city. There would be immigrants in offices cleaning and young people coming out of warehouses where they'd been dancing.

And then there was me going into that big old house from a hundred years ago.

Talking talking talking

Trying to find some kind of thing in my mind, my memory — something.

When all the time it was my gut that was hurting. But oh no.

And we did.

I mean there was —

I told him about . . .

We did . . .

Oh this is so long ago . . .

It wasn't even my . . .

The time my father would cry about . . .

Hold me and cry about . . .

My father would cry about his grandfather who'd told him about . . .

The camp, you know.

Oh — my gut is still so — maybe a twinge — did I? — but actually, you know, miraculously still . . .

Still calm because . . .

That was the past. That was history. That was the last century.

That was so long ago. I'm not going to pretend that those emotions are my emotions just so just so — just so the —

He was a little shit, that man.

Little fat Jew.

Pain in the gut.

Oh. That shouldn't be happening.

This really shouldn't . . .

I've had no caffeine for, for . . . so many years . . . for three years.

Ooooo-uuughhh-ugggggghhhh.

ERRRRRRRRRR! AAGGGGHHHHH!

Oh God. Oh God. Oh God . . .

It's . . .

Shit. Fuck.

This should not be happening.

Ahh.

Long pause.

Better now.

I don't . . . why?

There's nothing to make that –

I shouldn't . . . a Jew is . . .

Jews are . . . wonderful. Jews are . . . people. You know.

Just the whole therapy thing, the whole . . . thing. It wasn't for
me.

I just sensed.

And when I read the – when I saw the magazine piece about
the caffeine intolerance, I just knew.

I thought: that's me.

I have to reconsider breakfast.

And I did.

And look at me now.

Serene.

It's not my word. It's the word several friends and colleagues
have used about me.

You are now a serene person.

Somebody even used the word: reborn.

So I suppose . . .

The shower's stopped. Thomas will be towelling himself.

Silence. Zachary has turned his DVD off. Zachary is getting dressed. Thomas is getting dressed.

My breakfast is complete.

Silence now.

Isn't that wonderful?

My gut is . . . my gut is . . . my gut is . . . so calm.

Look – a postcard from my downstairs neighbour writing from the rehab clinic. I didn't think they were allowed to do that.

She says she's writing to all the people she's hurt and wants to apologise.

She doesn't need forgiveness. But she wants us to know she's working on herself and is determined to be a new people. She means person.

I think I'll put it on the fridge with the spare magnet. Over there by Zachary's painting of the soldier with no head.

Of course, yes, I'd prefer it if his people had heads – but they don't. And that's just the way Zachary sees them. And that's the way he expresses himself.

Each of us is an individual. I won't judge.

She didn't need to do that. She really didn't.

A new person. Well, I look forward to that. She'll be welcome in here if she's no longer dependent. Zachary can read for her.

Thomas? Zachary?

Tom?

Zac?

Gone. No goodbye.

Well – it's late. There's a rush.

I say a little prayer: don't let them be bombed today.

We'll text later. And I'll remind Thomas about the theatre.

I'm going to get new shoes today.

I just feel like it.

UGH. MY STOMACH. I AM A SLAVE TO MY . . .

Such a fucking mystery.

Really thought I was going to be happy.

What can you do?

(I may have a frappa I mean fuck it just fuck it I may have a fucking frappawatsitcino whatfucking ever.)

When you've tried everything – Inga, the little Jew – everything – what can you do? What the the fuck can you do?

Well, there's war on, isn't there? It says on the telly so it must be – the war has begun. We've invaded them.

Now I have zinc and calcium and iron. It's quite a little ritual, isn't it?

But I think they do play a part in – they are doing a part in making my life –

As near as perfect as any life can be.

She takes the tablets.

Play Three

Women in Love

Anna, Dan.

Anna   It was the week after the chemo and the radio ended and you were in for observation and I said to you: I've brought you breakfast. I didn't know whether you wanted breakfast. I didn't know whether you were allowed breakfast. But I decided you should have breakfast.

Dan   And I said: Thank you for bringing me breakfast.

Anna   And I asked: Did you sleep at all? I want you to sleep.

Dan   And I said: I sleep all the time. They bring me drugs so I sleep all the time.

Anna   And I said: Well, that's good. I'm glad they bring you drugs so that you can sleep. It must be hard to sleep.

Dan   And I said: Oh yes. It's hard to sleep in here. People are mad or people are in pain so they call out in the night. Yes. Last night a woman called out that she was an angel with a broken wing.

Anna   I laughed.

Dan   You did. And I laughed. An angel with a broken wing. And she was lost and would God come and rescue her.

Anna   And I said: She'll be one of the mad ones then.

Dan   You did: One of the mad ones then.

Anna   There's coffee for your breakfast. And I handed you the coffee. It's from a machine. But that's all they had.

Dan   And I said: A machine is alright.

Anna   There's no sugar, I said.

Dan   And I said: I've got little packets of sugar. I found these. Because I like coffee very sweet. That's what I said.

Anna   And I said: I don't want you having sugar. You shouldn't, you know. Your body. Chemo. Radio. Sugar.

Dan   You did. But you gave me the stirrer.

Anna   Did I? Really? I don't remember the stirrer.

Dan   Oh yes, the stirrer. Definitely the stirrer.

Anna   That's a detail I've forgotten.

Dan   And you said: I'm sorry, it's broken.

Anna   Ah yes!

Dan/Anna   I'm sorry, it's broken, but that's the only one I have.

Both laugh.

Dan   Ah yes.

Anna   Ah yes. Of course I remember the stirrer now. And you poured all the sugar into your coffee.

Dan   I did. And I asked you if you'd brought a newspaper.

Anna   And I said no because a newspaper is too depressing and you won't get better if you're reading newspapers.

Dan   You did say that. And I was angry with you.

Anna   You were angry with me. Which wasn't good for you. And there was a croissant.

Dan   Which also came out of a machine and had a bit of chocolate in the middle.

Anna   I'm sorry I couldn't do any better. Plastic cup and (*laughs*) plastic croissant.

Dan   Ah well.

Anna   Ah well.

Dan   And I said: I need to see the news.

Anna   I said: No.

Dan   And I said: I saw the TV news last night. The invasion.

Anna   And I said: How?

Dan   I had the nurse bring the TV into my room on a trolley, I said.

Anna   The poof nurse? I asked.

Dan   Nancy the Nurse, yes, I replied. Nancy the Nurse wheeled the TV into my room and we watched the invasion on the news together. The desert.

Anna   I didn't have any breakfast myself that morning.

Dan   No you didn't.

Anna   No I didn't. And I said: Nancy Nurse fancies you.

Dan   Do you think so? I said.

Anna   I think so, I said. And I think you flirt with Nancy the Nurse, I said.

Dan   Well, maybe I do, I said, maybe I do.

Anna   Definitely you do, I said. Wheeling in the television. I don't want that to happen. You won't get better if that goes on.

Dan   I said: I like flirting.

Anna   You'll flirt with anything, I said.

Dan   Why else do you think we're together? I said.

Anna   And you reached out and stroked my breast.

Dan   No.

Anna   Oh yes.

Dan   No.

Anna   Yes, definitely yes.

Dan   Funny . . . I don't . . . no . . . no . . .

Anna   You did, I swear to . . . stroked my breast –

Dan   You're embellishing the –

Anna   No. No. No.

Dan   I had the strength? In my arm?

Anna   I suppose you must have done.

Dan   I didn't think I had the strength in my arm. Ah well. What did you feel?

Anna   Well . . .

Dan   Was there . . . ? Arousal?

Anna   Yes. Arousal. The nipple – erected.

Dan   How am I forgetting . . . ?

Anna   Some embarrassment of course. We were in a hospital room.

Dan   Well, fuck that.

Anna   And pride that I'd got you. I'd got you and Nancy the Nurse and the poofter persuasion weren't sticking their cocks / up you.

Dan   No thank you.

Anna   Well, that's how I lost Brendan –

Dan   Of course.

Anna   And relief that your arm could do that.

Dan   Miraculous.

Anna   And anger because you'd smeared chocolate from the croissant all over my top.

Dan   Choccy titties. (*Laughs.*)

Anna (*laughs*)   Choccy titties.

Dan   Mmmm. I said: I saw the TV news and on the TV news I saw – did you see the TV news last night?

Anna   Yes I saw the TV news last night, I said.

Dan   And on the TV news last night I saw the soldier have his head blown off. Did you see that?

Anna   And I told you: Yes I did see the soldier have his head blown off.

Dan   By the suicide bomber. Have you ever seen anything so horrific on your television?

Anna   No I haven't, I said.

Dan   No I haven't either, I said.

Anna   I said: You won't get better.

Dan   I really don't think I did touch your breast.

Anna   Oh yes oh yes. In fact . . . look. Same top. Chocolate still there. See. See.

Dan   My eyes are . . .

Anna   I've scrubbed and I've scrubbed . . .

Dan   My eyes are still . . .

Anna   But the stain won't come out.

Dan   Bring your choccy titty very close, my dear, bring choccy titty for inspection.

Anna   Can you see that now?

Dan   I think so. Maybe a little closer.

Enter **Rusty**.

Rusty   Can I have the TV now?

Anna   Said Nancy the Nurse.

Rusty   The old bitch next door's got a ticket. Her son brings her a ticket with her winning numbers on twice a week.

Anna   Said Nancy the Nurse.

Rusty   It's rollover today and she reckons she's gonna win thirty million. I said to her: What's the point of thirty million, Grandma? The doctors have only given you another week to live, and she says to me: You got to have hope, son, you gotta hope, son.

Dan   And Nancy the Nurse unplugged the television from the wall.

Rusty   I don't know. Is that good? Hoping for thirty million when you've got seven more days on this planet or is it just plain fucking stupid? I throw it out as a question.

Dan   Pondered Nancy the Nurse.

Anna   And out he went with the television. She had the television on very loud next door.

Dan   Did she?

Anna   Oh yes. Don't you remember that?

Dan   No.

Anna   She had the rollover on very loud next door. She was a very old lady.

Dan   I see. I asked you: Were there pictures of the soldier with his head blown off on the cover of this morning's paper?

Anna   And I said: I'm not telling you. I'm not talking about it. I'm not talking about it. And I gave you extra pills: vitamins. Minerals. Zinc. Calcium.

Dan   I had a lot of pills rattling around inside me.

Anna   You did, and I stuffed more down you, but I really, I really – we all have to supplement our diets, you know? We're not getting enough goodness / when when –

Dan   Coffee and croissants from a machine.

Anna   Exactly. Exactly.

Dan   For breakfast.

Anna   It's killing us. Really, so just –

Dan   And I took all the tablets you gave me.

Anna   You did.

Dan   And you kissed me on the lips.

Anna   Did I?

Dan Oh yes. Always a kiss on the lips after I've taken my pills. You always do it.

Anna Do I?

Dan Without thinking about it, yes, you always do. I love you.

Anna And I love you. Totally. Sometimes I wish I didn't. But I do. I love you totally.

Dan Thank you.

Anna With all my, my, my . . .

Dan Choccy tits.

Anna With all my choccy tits, yes.

Dan Choccy tits. Sugar lips and a candyfloss cunt.

Anna I'm a sugary girl.

Dan And I said: Let's talk about the university

Anna And I said: Oh no oh no oh no.

Dan Oh yes oh yes oh yes.

Anna No work until you're better –

Dan Yes yes yes yes yes yes yes yes yes yes –

Anna We're not – no – talking about work until you're better. I said that: I said that, no no no. You will not get better, I said, you will not get better if you are worrying about the university.

Dan And I said: There is no point. Don't you understand? There is no point in getting better if there is not the university, don't you see that? Don't you see? Yes I'm here yes I'm ill yes I'm probably here because of the university, I'm not stupid, I can see that my whole life the stress the pressure the time wasted to make this has made me an ill person but also it's the I am that person and there is nothing there is nothing there is nothing.

Anna You won't, you won't, I care, I said. I love you. I'm here. I live in a hospital because I love you and you – you love the university YES YOU FUCKING DO – you fucking love this thing and I'm a person and I –

But now it was suddenly written on the wall in front:

> ONLY WOMEN LOVE. MEN DO SOMETHING –
> THERE'S A THING GOING ON THAT'S CLOSE TO . . .
> MEN HAVE A FEELING. BUT ONLY WOMEN *LOVE*.
> AND YOU WILL GIVE AND HE WILL NEVER . . .
> LIKE A WHALE FLYING TO THE MOON.

Dan   I'm listening to this.

Anna   I know. And . . . ?

Dan   And it's very interesting.

Anna   So of course you, any man, can achieve, of course they can do, of course they've done all this stuff in the world, they've done everything because they don't feel –

Dan   All I asked was that we talk about the university.

Anna   This fucking awful burden of love cut it out. That's the curse. If ever there was a . . . tree of knowledge . . . Eve . . . the apple . . . blah . . . if ever there was the curse . . . this LOVE thing . . . cut it . . .

Dan   Shhh. I kiss you and I say I love you.

Anna   You do. You do. You do. And I kiss you and say I love you.

Dan   So where's the . . . ?

Anna   Sorry. Forgive me. I was unfair.

Dan   I have feelings. Just they don't always . . .

Anna   Hey. Candyflosschocolatelemonade, sir?

Dan   Tell me about the university, I said.

Anna   Alright, I said, maybe we'll do that. A little bit of talk about the university would be alright. I don't want you turning this room into your office.

Dan   I won't. I promise, I said.

Anna   Alright, I said.

Anna   Your eyes were starting to close then.

Dan   No. I don't think so.

Anna   Oh yes. Your head was falling back on the pillow. Your eyes were closing. Your breath . . . it rasped.

Dan   Continue with the research.

Anna   And your head fell back.

And there was silence then.

The lottery had finished in the next room.

And you lay there and the time passed. I put your research away.

Enter **Rusty**.

Anna   Did she win the thirty million? I asked you.

Rusty   She lost her ticket. She can't remember her numbers. She's very old, I replied.

Anna   And I said: Oh well.

Rusty   I told you: She's weeping. I could be a very rich woman and not know it. They'll rollover if I don't claim my prize.

I said to her: You didn't win. Give up, Grandma. Just be happy you've got no memory.

I wish I had no memory.

Anna   I write everything down at the end of the day.

Rusty   And I said: Let it go, dear, let it . . .

People come. They fuck you. You fuck them. You move on. You let them go.

And diseases carry them away and you move on.

Anna   And you? I asked.

Rusty (*laughs*)   I'm blown up, bomb on a bus on the way home tonight, I replied. I go out through the window in a ball of flames. Flaming. Screaming. My life.

Anna (*checking* **Dan**)   Is he alright? He's . . . rasping.

Rusty   He's not doing too badly. He'll be out of here. You should go home. When did you get here?

Anna   Nine-something. Breakfast.

Rusty   Midnight now. Fifteen fucking hours. You go home.

Anna   I'm going to sleep here.

Rusty   His wife phoned, I told you. You didn't like that.

Anna   No: I was fine about that. I've met his wife. We shared a coffee. We're . . . we understand each other now. I asked you: Is there no one in your life?

Rusty   Oh yes, I replied. When he's on leave. He's in the invasion force.

I always wanted a soldier, since I was seven, and now I got one.

Sometimes it's bad. I fart. He thinks it's a landmine.

He gets nightmares. Suicide bombers. I hold him. It's a war on terror, isn't it?

Anna   Do you watch the news? I asked. Don't let him [*Dan*] watch the news.

Rusty   And I said: I keep an eye out. But − I don't. I'm not stupid about this. He won't be forever.

Anna   And I said: I'm stupid.

Rusty   How much do you love him?

Anna   Everything.

Rusty   You shouldn't. It hurts.

Anna   I know.

Rusty   Yeah.

Screams, off.

Listen, I told you. Listen, she's started again.

Anna   'Oh forgive me, Father, forgive me. My wing has broken and I'm alone in Paradise. I followed Lucifer and that was wrong and take me back.'

Rusty   We laughed: Mad.

Anna   Mad.

Rusty   Listen, I offered. I can smuggle you – don't tell anyone – but there's a couple of spare temazepams. It's hard to sleep in here, I said.

Anna   No thank you, I said. I prefer not to – Western medicine, I said.

Rusty   Uh-huh, I said. And all through the night that woman screamed out for her broken wing and you slept in that chair and there was no bomb to take me away and no news from the the theatre of war and –

Anna   And each of us made it through the night and the morning came and we carried on.

Exit **Rusty**.

Anna   I brought you breakfast – from a machine.

Dan   I love you.

Anna   I know.

Dan   I mean it. Did you bring sugar? I'll need sugar.

Anna   No news today. Nothing happened in the world today. Nothing. Okay? Nothing at all. (*Kisses him.*) And I love you.

Play Four

Fear and Misery

Kitchen. **Harry**, **Olivia**. *They are eating supper. We hear a child's sleeping breath on a baby monitor.*

Harry Do you remember the night Alex was conceived?

Olivia Of course.

Harry Were you calm? That night.

Olivia Calm? Why do you . . . ?

Harry Well . . . Sometimes I wonder if you were really . . . It's important to me that my boy was conceived in total . . .

Olivia Well . . .

Harry As I planned it.

Olivia As you planned . . . Really? Why is it always − ? It doesn't matter. It doesn't matter − Alex was conceived.

Harry In calm. Say it. In . . . Tell me he was conceived in calm.

Olivia Listen . . . it doesn't . . . I love you.

Harry So why can't you . . . ? Whatever it is. Listen. Whatever. We say . . .

Olivia This is . . . It's okay.

Harry Really . . .

Olivia I'm opening some . . . (*wine*). Would you . . . ?

Harry You had to be calm. That's important.

Olivia Well . . . well . . . actually . . . actually . . . I wasn't.

Harry Oh . . . oh. No?

Olivia Sorry.

Harry   Tell me.

Olivia   I can't.

Harry   Tell me. TELL ME. FUCKING WELL – Partners? Partners tell – That is a – you tell me.

Olivia   Well . . .

Pours two glasses. They drink for some time.

Sometimes I'm . . . Sometimes . . . you're inside me. We're . . . making love. We really are . . . making love. But it feels like, it seems like – there's a sort of . . . rape. Sorry. Rape. Sorry. Rape. Sorry.

Long pause.

Harry   Ever been raped?

Olivia   No.

Harry   Ever fantasised about being raped?

Olivia   No!

Harry   So why the fuck, why the fuck, why the . . . spoil the moment our child was conceived? Spoil the . . . In this world of fear why spoil the one . . .

Olivia   Sometimes your eyes like – it's a moment, it's nothing.

Harry   I'm a good man. I'm a kind man.

Olivia   A moment like you don't want to make love but instead make – hate – make . . . like you want to . . .

Harry   Were you ever abused? Your father?

Olivia   There are moments in the past when I've felt for a blink there's a blink of . . . rape and then it's back to love again.

Harry   Do I scare you now?

Olivia   No.

Harry   What are you feeling now?

Olivia   Sorry I said anything. Sorry. I love you – respect you – trust you – I totally totally love you. I do I do I do I do.

Harry   Listen – you're my refuge.

Olivia   And you're . . .

Harry   Cuddle.

She does.

The world out there is so . . . somehow, somehow, when my back was turned, somehow the world turned so bad. And when I come back to you . . .

Olivia   You're keeping us safe here. I know that. I really – I appreciate – my love . . .

Harry   It's nothing. When was the last time the battery was checked on that smoke alarm?

He gets on a chair and removes the batteries.

Olivia   The security. The extra locks. The child locks. Making sure no plug is free. Keeping the mice at bay. I know the work you –

Harry   It's nothing.

Olivia   You work so hard to keep us out of harm's way and I thank you for that.

Harry   These things have to be done.

Olivia   I know, but still . . .

Harry   I'll change these. To be on the safe side. Will we make love tonight?

Olivia   I think we probably will. Yes. We will.

Harry   Will you trust me totally and utterly? Can you promise me there'll be no fear at all?

Olivia   . . . No. I can't.

Harry   Then maybe we won't make love.

Olivia   Alright.

Harry   Other men'd fuck you harder, fuck you harder, smash you harder and then you'd know it's rape, you know that, don't you? Don't you? You think it's rape with me –

Olivia   I don't think it's –

Harry   Then you can bet your fucking bottom fucking dollar that it's more like fucking rape with any other fucking man. OTHER MEN WOULD –

Olivia   QUIET. Shhh. Shhhh now, Alex is sleeping. Alex only got off . . . Quiet. I just got Alex off twenty minutes ago.

Harry   Sorry sorry sorry.

Olivia   It's really important Alex doesn't –

Harry   Of course of course of course. Is he alright? Did he seem alright?

Olivia   I think so, yes.

Harry   Any dreams?

Olivia   Not yet. It's early. He might still . . .

Harry   You didn't let him watch the news? The invasion.

Olivia   Of course not.

Harry   It's very important he doesn't – that's where he got this whole – the soldier dream, the thing, he got that from the news –

Olivia   Listen to him breathing.

Baby monitor. Breathing.

Sounds like he's doing alright to me.

Harry   Yes. He's alright. And what about us? Are we alright?

Olivia   (*laughs*)   Let's get pissed.

Harry   If we're frightened of each other . . .

Olivia   I'm not . . . no. Honestly. No.

Harry What frightens you?

Olivia Well . . .

Harry Hold you.

He does.

Olivia I go to the supermarket and suddenly a woman falls to the floor and says that God has banished her from Heaven and she's broken her wing. She's calling out to me: HELP ME HELP HELP ME OR I WILL HANG MYSELF FROM A TREE! How did that happen? I ran a bath with oils, I lit candles, but still that woman won't . . .

Harry Was Alex there – in the supermarket. Was Alex there?

Olivia Alex was with the childminder.

Harry It's just . . . it's just . . . it's just . . . it's just . . . it's just I think it's so important we keep Alex away from all these terrible things, you know? I can't bear to think of Alex being exposed –

Olivia He wasn't, he wasn't, he wasn't there, he was . . . he was playing while I was . . . It was terribly disturbing.

Harry But you're over it?

Olivia I suppose so.

Harry Shall we go out with our wine and sit on the bench?

Olivia The baby alarm doesn't work on the . . .

Harry Ah well then, ah well.

Olivia I really think we have to . . .

Harry Of course.

Pause.

Olivia Do I ever frighten you?

Harry Hah! You've never raped me.

Olivia   No, but . . . what do you − ? What scares you about
me?

Harry   That you won't wash your vagina. That you'll fuck a
black man. That you'll have a breast removed.

Olivia   . . . God.

Harry   I'm being honest.

Olivia   Okay.

Harry   Maybe I shouldn't have been . . .

Olivia   I really never −

Harry   YOU CALLED ME A FUCKING RAPIST FOR
FUCK'S SAKE. YOU TOLD ME MY SON WAS BORN
BECAUSE OF AN ACT OF RAPE.

Olivia   I DIDN'T. I DIDN'T. I NEVER DID THAT. I
NEVER DID. WON"T YOU − LEAVE IT, JUST LEAVE IT.
JUST LEAVE IT . . . Our child was born in love and
tranquillity and his life will be lived, he will never know, I will
do everything I can to make sure he never knows the fear and
− that I −

Harry   That we −

Olivia   We, we have known. We will work together. Keep
away from the addicts. The madwomen. The bombers. The
soldier with his head blown off. We will keep them away − yes?

Harry   Yes.

They stop, listen.

Olivia   . . . He's sleeping very well.

Harry   Yes.

They embrace.

Olivia   I want Alex to be clever but not so clever that he isn't
liked by other children. I want him to fall in love.

Harry   A girl −

Olivia   Or . . . whatever. I want him to be fulfilled. But above all . . .

Harry   Secure?

Olivia   Secure.

Harry   Yes. Secure.

Olivia   Security is the most important thing in this life.

Harry   It is. I want to be with you forever.

Olivia   And I with you.

Harry   Do you mean that, do you really really really mean that?

Olivia   Idiot. I wash my vagina obsessively. I've never fucked a black man. And my tits are staying put.

Harry   Don't belittle me.

Olivia   Oh please.

Harry   The gypsies are finally moving on. There's been a police thing and they've finally moved the gypsies on.

Olivia   Well, that's good.

Harry   So that's one less bunch to set the car alarm off.

Olivia   Great great. I'm getting a bit sleepy. Early breakfast tomorrow.

Harry   I thought we could make love tonight.

Olivia   Let's see, okay?

Harry   Okay. If you're not sure . . .

Olivia   Alex has pre-school Latin at seven thirty so –

Harry   Of course. Listen, if you want to go to bed. I just want to . . . I need to finish these smoke alarms.

Olivia   I see.

Harry   It's been three months since I last . . . we could burn up in the night. That's one of my worst – this old . . . that

we all just burn away in the night. I can't sleep sometimes
because . . .

Olivia   You never said.

Harry   Well . . .

Olivia   You should tell me.

Harry   I do, but you're sleeping and I –

Olivia   Still. Tell me. I'll be washing extra hard tonight.
Down there.

Harry   Sorry I said that.

Olivia   Is my body so frightening? You're frightened of this?
My vagina, my tits, my – fear fear fear.

Harry   Here we go. Here we go. Here we go. RAPIST.
RAPIST. RAPIST.

Olivia   SHUT UP. SHUT UP. SHUT UP SHUT THE
FUCK UP.

Alex *murmurs in his sleep.*

Olivia   Oh God, have we – ?

Harry   I'll check on him.

Exit **Harry**. **Olivia** *spots estate agent's details. Reads them.* **Harry**
re-enters.

Harry   He's asleep.

Olivia   Well . . .

Harry   Everything's okay.

Olivia   Well . . .

Harry   The crack house was raided last night.

Olivia   Oh good.

Harry   We were talking in the – buying my paper – and the
police bust their way, exploded it open and rounded them all
up and now the bastards are waiting trial. Let's pray it's prison.

Olivia   Well, that's good news.

Harry   Isn't it? Isn't it? Isn't it? I'm sorry if I . . .

Olivia   Doesn't matter.

Harry   I do love you.

Olivia   I know.

Harry   I do love you and I want you to love me. Shall we go to bed? Good for property prices. Gyppos moved on. Crackheads moved on. This place is going to rocket.

Olivia   You think so?

Harry   Oh yes, you just watch, this place is just going to totally rocket.

Olivia   We're sitting on a fortune?

Harry   A wise investment. But still, I'm not sure this place, this street, this whole −

Olivia   But . . . Character, history, community −

Harry   Yes, I know

Olivia   Character, history, community − we said, agreed.

Harry   But still I'm not sure. This was fun for us. This was . . . colour. The poor, the ethnics, the, the . . .

Olivia   Gyppos on crack.

Harry   Exactly. Exactly. Exactly. Exactly. The gippos on crack. I'm not sure all that − for Alex, for Alex for Alex's future, for the security, for the security of Alex's future.

Olivia   What's this? (*Estate agent's details.*) This was on the . . .

Harry   I printed it off the . . . A new community. Gated community. Good catchment area.

Olivia   A new-build?

Harry   I was just surfing. I think we should consider −

Olivia   I don't want a new-build. You know what I want, know what I want and still you go ahead −

Harry   I was just curious about the possibility.

Olivia   Without even talking to me you go ahead –

Harry   I want I want for fuck's sake, fuck's sake, look around you, look, look – there's . . . they are selling heroin at the station, they are in gangs on buses, they have knives, they are fighting on the streets and now and now and now there are bombs. How can you be – ? How can you wilfully . . . ? It's fucking frightening, it's so fucking –

Olivia   I know, I know.

Harry   And now when I explore, when I think about the possibility, you just –

Olivia   I have to sleep.

Harry   Walk down the street and your eyes are scanning, scanning, never meeting a gaze of course because that would be . . . but scanning. Waiting for the blow to come. The . . . something. Kick in the gut. Bullet in the head. But somehow knowing it will . . . Knowing that, knowing that's . . . inevitable. Knowing that 'they' will attack you. They will steal from you, bully you, humiliate you. They will. They will.

A **Soldier** *covered in blood and mud enters and watches* **Harry** *and* **Olivia***. They can't see him.*

Harry   I want us – you, me, Alex – to build a wall against . . . Somehow the world out there got full of . . . Somehow there's nothing but hate out there. Aggression. Somehow the streets got filled with addicts who need to steal to get so high they can kill who then come down and want to attack and steal your . . . THE WORLD IS ATTACKING US, THE TERROR IS EATING US UP AND YOU . . . WE NEED GATES. WE NEED TO, TO, TO . . . DRAW UP THE DRAWBRIDGE AND CLOSE THE GATES AND SECURITY, SECURITY, SECURITY, SECURITY. I CAN'T FIGHT THIS WAR EVERY DAY. WAR WITH THE SCUM. THE POOR, POOR DRUG-HUNGRY MENTALLY DERANGED DAMAGED SCUM. I HAVE TO HAVE PEACE. I'M NORMAL. YOU'RE – ALEX WILL BE GIFTED AND

WE CAN'T CARRY GUNS EVERY DAY. WE CAN'T.
SOMEWHERE JUST TO GROW. WE'VE EARNED
THAT. WE WORK.

*The **Soldier** turns and exits to go to **Alex**.*

Harry   WE ARE LOVING – AND I WANT THIS.
I WANT THESE GATES. I WANT TO FEEL SAFE
BEHIND THESE GATES. THIS IS THE ONLY WAY
I WILL FEEL SAFE. BEHIND THESE GATES. SO
DON"T YOU – COMMUNITY, THAT'S A LIE.
THERE'S NO COMMUNITY. I HAVE NO COMMUNITY
WITH THEM. I WILL FIGHT FOR THIS, I –

Alex *screams.*

Olivia   You – Don't you – no – Alex – No, I'm going to him.
You – PRICK.

She goes.

(*Off.*) Come on, sweetheart, come on, I'm here, Mummy's
here, alright, Mummy's here to hold you, yes, that's right. Did
you see the soldier, yes? Oh no. Was he missing his head like . . .
yes? Yes, darling, there is a war but it's not our war, we don't . . .
There are some of our soldiers, yes, but we don't even . . . we
don't want that war to happen and it's a long way away, that
war is such a long, long, long way away. Okay? Okay? We're . . .
Are you going to go to sleep for Mummy? Will you do that?
Good boy, Alex. Night. Night.

She enters. Sits. Long pause. **Olivia** *looks at the estate agent's details.*

Olivia   Well . . . maybe.

Harry   Yes?

Olivia   Maybe.

Harry   Look. I did some sums. If we do a week less in the
Dordogne, we could rent this place out, the maths is looking
pretty –

Olivia   Can I look at them in bed?

Harry   Okay.

Olivia   I'll read it all before lights out. I know. I think maybe you're right, maybe Alex will – maybe a more stable environment.

Harry   You reckon?

Olivia   It's got to, yes – somewhere safer might – he might stop having those terrible – the gated thing might do that.

Harry   I think it might. But if I'm raping you . . .

Olivia   No. Nothing. A few blinks.

Harry   The night Alex was born?

Olivia   No. I'm sure not. Alex was conceived with love.

Harry   That's important.

Olivia   Can we go to bed?

Harry   Let's.

Play Five

War and Peace

Alex, Soldier.

Alex   And Alex was seven and Alex said to the soldier: Why do you come here?

Soldier   And the soldier had no head.

Alex   Why?

Soldier   And the soldier said: . . . I'm sorry, son.

Alex   I don't like you, said Alex.

Soldier   I know, said the soldier.

Alex   So – just . . .

Soldier   I have to, the soldier said.

Alex   But Alex said: You're disgusting. You're horrible. Look at you. Ugh.

Soldier   Soldier said: I know that, son, don't you think I fucking know that? I fucking know how fucking horrible I am. If I could have my head back again –

Alex   Leave me alone, Alex said. I'm perfect.

Soldier   My girl's fucking left. My mates in the regiment's gone off, said the soldier.

Alex   And Alex said: I'm a perfect child.

Soldier   Soldier – I'm . . . it is so horrible. I've been kicking mirrors and windows and that.

Alex   Alex – Look at you – blood.

Soldier   That is very, very, very old blood. Nothing fresh on me.

Alex   I thought you weren't coming tonight, said Alex.

Soldier   Couldn't keep away, said the soldier.

Alex   Mum and Dad are downstairs, said Alex.

Soldier   And the soldier said: I really want to talk to you. Need to talk to you.

Alex   I could call for them, said Alex.

Soldier   You could –

Alex   Maybe I'll do that. Maybe I will – 'Mum, Dad.'

Soldier   No don't don't don't. Our time, okay? Our time? You told me you liked our time?

Alex   Sometimes.

Soldier   And other . . . ?

Alex   I'm frightened sometimes, Alex told the soldier with no head. He told the soldier with no head: I wee the bed. Last time. Other times.

Soldier   I didn't know that, said the soldier.

Alex   I'm talking to a . . . it's a psychiatrist.

Soldier   What do you tell them?

Alex   Not much.

Soldier   So this is our secret?

Alex   Oh yes.

Soldier   Let's keep it that way, yeah?

Alex   And Alex told the soldier: I draw pictures of you. They think you're a dream. They don't know . . .

Soldier   We agreed this was a secret, said the soldier.

Alex   I know.

Soldier   I'm keeping my side of the bargain, you keeping yours? Yes? Yes?

Alex   Yes, said Alex.

Soldier   Good boy, said the soldier. That is – oh good on you, son, yes yes yes, good boy.

Alex   And Alex said: I am a good boy, everyone says so. What do you do?

Soldier   Girl won't have me. So I sleep in an alleyway, soldier said. Wank and sleep.

Alex   Sounds horrid.

Soldier   The army – it toughens you up, said the soldier. I've seen worse. And then the soldier asked: Can I touch your head again?

Alex   But Alex said: You smell of alleyway.

Soldier   But the soldier said: I really want to . . . tonight . . . I really want to touch your head tonight, son.

Alex   But Alex said: You're so dirty.

Soldier   And the soldier said: Do I look like a monster to you?

Alex   Yes, said Alex.

Soldier   And the soldier said: Fear's okay. That's a good thing, fear is. I've been been scared so many times.

Alex   Yeah?

Soldier   Oh yeah. So many times. Made me a man. I've shat my pants twenty times a day and still carried on fighting. And the soldier said: Join the army, son. No one's a man till they join the army. And he said: I'm just – a bloke, yeah?

Alex   But Alex said: You got no head.

Soldier   Lost fighting the fight . . .

Alex   Which fight? I want to understand the fight. Who are the enemies?

Soldier   But the soldier said: Please. Let me feel your head again. Such a good head. You're a fine lad.

Alex　I'm outstanding. Everyone says so.

Soldier　I'm sure they do and I'm a piece of shit. Oh son, let me touch you.

Alex　Can I hold your gun? asked Alex.

Soldier　After.

Alex　I want to do it now. I play with your gun while you touch my head.

Soldier　That's not what we usually . . .

Alex　I know. But still . . .

Soldier　And the soldier said to Alex: Like the feel of my gun, huh?

Alex　Yeah.

Soldier　Feel like a big man, yeah?

Alex　Yeah.

Soldier　We're all the same: big man with a gun in your hand. How old are you?

Alex　Seven.

Soldier　And then the soldier said: Too young to know it. But you wait – few years you'll feel empty, empty, aching all day, like you lost yourself a long time ago.

Alex　But Alex said: My life is good.

Soldier　Empty, he said. But you always feel finished with this [*gun*] in your hand. Live without food, live without money – you can do it, it's hard but you do it. Live without family, live without friends – that's easy. But live without war? No human being's ever done that. Never will. It's what makes us human.

Alex　Who you killed? asked Alex.

Soldier　Towelhead. Coming for me so . . . Kid only a few years older than you but he's coming towards me with a gun so . . . phut.

Alex　Was that good?

Soldier   It was alright.

Alex   Alex – Give me the gun.

Soldier   Soldier – I gotta touch your head.

Alex   Alex – Gun first. Gun gun gun gun gun gun gun gun.

Soldier   Soldier – You drive a hard deal, don't you? You're a deal driver, son.

Alex   I want to be in the City like my mummy and daddy, said Alex.

Soldier   Do you? Do you? Do you? I can see that, yes.

Alex   Gun.

Soldier   You keep the deal we . . . There you go.

He gives **Alex** *the gun.*

Alex   It's a heavy one.

Soldier   There's heavier than that. Like it?

Alex   Oh yeah.

Soldier   What will you do in the City?

Alex   Hedge funds.

Soldier   I don't know much about –

Alex   They're high-yielding.

Soldier   What a strange little bloke you are.

Alex   No, said Alex.

Soldier   I've got to touch you, son, okay, okay? I gave you my – okay?

Alex   Okay.

Soldier *touches* **Alex**'s *head.*

Soldier   And the soldier said: Beautiful hair. Skin. Teeth like . . . These teeth are so fucking good . . . You go to a dentist, we never used to go to a dentist. And he said: You got such a fine head. So beautiful.

Alex   I know, said Alex.

Soldier   One day the girls are gonna fight over you.

Alex   I suppose, said Alex.

Soldier   Oh they will, believe me, son, they will. Girls go for all this. You want a girl?

Alex   Later.

Soldier   That's it. Plenty of time for pussy, yeah? Plenty of time for pussy. Oh yeah . . .

Alex   Will you stop touching me soon? asked Alex.

Soldier   Uh-huh.

Alex   I'd like that, said Alex.

Soldier   You keep playing with that gun. My fingers are disgusting, are they?

Alex   Yes.

Soldier   But you like me, yeah? We're friends, yeah? You told me we were friends?

Alex   I don't know.

Soldier   You told me, son.

Alex   I suppose.

Soldier   You're my only friend in the world. I need you. These nights we have, our secret nights, these are everything I've got.

Alex   I know.

Soldier   So don't you – you got a bit of snot, I'll wipe you.

Alex   It's alright. I don't –

Soldier   I'll wipe you. (*Wipes.*) See, that's alright? That's alright now, isn't it? That's perfect now. The head's just perfect now. We got to look after this head, yeah?

Alex   Yeah. And then Alex asked: Do you want it?

Soldier   What's that?

Alex   Is that why you come here? asked Alex.

Soldier   What you talking about?

Alex   Do you come here, said Alex, because you want my head?

Soldier   The soldier said: You're a mad crazy little kid, aren't you?

Alex   Alex said: I'm a clever boy. I've worked it out. Night after night. You come in. You walk through my wall. Night after night. You want my head.

Soldier   No. Have you told anyone else?

Alex   You want to take my head away, yes yes yes?

Soldier   Oh son –

Alex   You want to take my head and put it on you and go away, that's what you want to do.

Soldier   Son, please –

Alex   I know what you're – well, no no no no no.

Soldier   I need a head.

Alex   Not mine.

Soldier   It's a beauty.

Alex   It's for me. It's for my life. My perfect life. It's not for you.

Soldier   I'm in agony, son. I'm needing I'm wanting a . . . oh please, son –

Alex   MUMMY! MUMMY! DADDY!

Soldier   Oh no, don't you, don't you – I'm bigger than you, I'm a big man with training and –

Alex   DADDY!

Soldier   No, son, don't you fucking −

Soldier *covers* **Alex***'s mouth.*

Soldier   Listen, son, okay, listen, you listen to what I got to say, this world this country this . . . everything exists because of me, because I go out there and I fight the fucking towelheads.

Alex   Mmmmgggguh.

Soldier   And if we can't fight them fucking towelheads then this is over, right − yeah? Yeah? This place, gated community, hedge funds, that's over unless I'm fighting the fighting. You see? You see? You see?

Alex *bites the* **Soldier***'s hand.* **Soldier** *pulls away.*

Soldier   You little fucker. Fucking bit me, you −

Alex   Could have shot you, said Alex.

Soldier   Yeah.

Alex   Boom! said Alex.

Soldier   Yeah.

Alex   You bleeding? said Alex

Soldier   Some, said the soldier.

Alex   Show me.

Soldier   No head − I can't fight, I can't . . .

Alex   SHOW ME.

Soldier *raises hand.*

Alex   Lots. I did that.

Soldier   You proud?

Alex   Oh yes. And Alex said: We want to keep people like you out. Gated community. That's us.

Soldier   You keep me out? You'd like that?

Alex   Maybe.

Soldier   Soldier in your room every night. You wouldn't stop that? Would you? Would you? Would you?

Alex   . . . I don't know.

Soldier   Think this is all yours, but you know, you know . . . See all this? This wasn't always gates. Oh no. This was mine, the soldier said.

Alex   Yeah? said Alex.

Soldier   All this was – there was no gates when I was a kid, when I was your age, fifteen years ago. This was an estate, said the soldier. This was all council, far as the eye could see, beautiful that was, beautiful. Few Asians. They were alright. And we'd play up and down the streets. And we'd play war. Beautiful it was. You stop when your mum called 'Tea' then you'd go out and you'd kill and bomb and landmine till the sun went down and then you'd go into bed and you'd sleep so sound. See my estate? And now . . . Now? My estate. Wiped away. Half of them work in the shopping park. Half of us are freeing the world from the towelheads. Come on. Come on. Come on. Make me happy. Give me your fucking head. Yeah? Please. Yeah? What do you say?

Alex   I . . . I . . . I . . . And Alex pissed the bed.

Soldier   Pissed yourself?

Alex   Not as much as before. And Alex said: Go away now.

Soldier   I need a month, said the soldier. Give me your head for a month. A tour of duty. I hate this world. I get restless. Fight the big fight.

Alex   Alex said: No. Go away.

Soldier   I got to fight. You got to help me. You want your world? You want this life? Want this to go on forever? Then give me the head so I can fight.

Alex   I don't want to – Get back. No. No. No!

Alex *moves away.*

Soldier   And the soldier called out: I've been fighting. I want my reward. You took my estate. I'm fighting for your freedom and democracy . . . I'm fighting for democracy, least you can do is –

Alex   And Alex was angry and he shouted: You keep away from me, wanker. You – you – this is my room, this is my property, my family's . . . I do well in all the SATs . . . I'm gifted . . . We drive an SUV . . . I am so powerful and you're, you're . . . you're scum . . . you eat bad food, you have numeracy and literacy issues, you will never be on the property ladder, you smoke and play the lottery, you're dirt and you don't belong in a gated community. Out, get out, away. You are a monster. You look like a . . . you are a deformed monster. Monster / monster monster monster monster MONSTER MONSTER.

Soldier   Yeah, I'm fucking disgusting, what you gonna fucking do about it? Huh? Huh? Huh? Huh?

Alex   You make me feel sick. And Alex told the soldier: My piss is turning cold on the bed now. You're not human. I am human. But you're not human.

Soldier   I know, said the soldier.

Alex   My world is a safe world and I can't have you in it. My emotional needs.

Soldier   And the soldier said: Fuck you. I am this country. I love this country. I've got a job to do and I'm going to do it. And there's no little cunting kid and his fucking hedge fund going to stop me, see, because all this, this is worth nothing if we're not out there beating the towelheads, then, see, see, see? And the soldier said: GIVE ME THE HEAD!

Alex   Off me. Help!

Soldier   And the soldier held Alex's head and he pulled and he said: I'm never giving this head back, see? I'm going to keep this head for ever. You know what was wrong with wars before? They ended. There was peace. But this one goes on and on and on. It's a war on terror and it goes on and on and

on and on. There's no God, see? There's no end day. There's
just this war on terror on and on and on and on and on and
on and on and on and on and on and and on and on and on
and on and on and on and on and on and on and on and on
and and on and on and on and on. What's that? Hah! Hah! Oh
good boy, oh good lad. That's it. You shat yourself. Shit
everywhere. Hah hah hah hah hah hah hah.

Alex   Fuck off. Cunt.

He fires the gun, shoots the **Soldier** *in the arm.*

Soldier   Fuck. Agh.

He falls. **Alex** *kneels.*

Alex   Is there blood? asked Alex.

Soldier   Coming now.

Alex   Sorry, I just want a – do you want a plaster?

Soldier   That's no fucking good, son. That's as much use as
a cunt on a camel. FUCK. FUCK. CUNT FUCK PAIN
FUCK.

Alex (*raising gun*)   Don't swear in my room. My rules.

Soldier   Sorry.

Alex   I'm sorry I hurt you. . . . See this house? Such a good
investment. Be worth a million before you know it. You should
go. You don't belong in a gated community – Ugh. You're . . .
blood on my duvet now.

Soldier   And my brains are blown across the desert.

Alex   So hard to get cleaners. There's the work. But they're
lazy. (*Gun pointed.*) I want you to go now. Go away. Now, or I'll
shoot you in the chest. Thank you for coming.

Soldier   It's a hard life, son. But maybe you'll never know
that.

Alex   And Alex told the soldier: I'm going to retire when I'm
fifty.

Soldier   You're a wanker. I'm a cunt.

Alex   You're rude.

Soldier   I'm a man, said the soldier, and then he said:
Goodbye.

Alex   And the soldier went but Alex kept his gun. And the
war went on.

Play Six

Yesterday an Incident Occurred

A group of **Speakers**.

–   Good morning/evening.

–   Yesterday there was an assault in this space. An incident occurred of a violent nature.

–   If you saw that incident we ask you to come forward, come forward and make yourself known.

–   We will respect your rights at all time.

–   Your privacy will be protected.

    But please come forward –

–   Yes. You have rights. Of course you have rights. But you have responsibilities as well.

–   Not reporting, not coming forward, witnessing and not coming forward to report a violent offence is something we take very seriously indeed.

–   Very seriously indeed.

–   Very seriously indeed.

–   You are a responsible citizen. I'm an optimist. I'm a philanthropist. I believe that most of us are inherently good. Most of us are doing our bit for those around us in a way that is inherently good.

–   But there's always the rotten egg.

–   Always there stinking in the barrel.

–   I am a caring person. I care deeply.

–   But we will not tolerate assaults upon our actors, our backstage staff or our front-of-house staff.

–   Why should we? Why should we? Why should we? Why should we?

–   Such attacks, assaults, attacks – by the rotten eggs – are entirely unacceptable.

–   Yesterday a member of the audience stepped forward, stepped forward out of his – it was a man – stepped forward and struck one of our cast members about the head. Our colleague fell to the floor. The audience member kicked him in a frenzy of, kicked him . . . Bones were broken, there was severe bruising, bleeding, internally and externally. The skull was fractured.

–   I was there. I was sharing a scene – it was utterly horrible.

–   We live in a time of terror, of random, violent, horrible, random, pointless attacks. There is a war on. Abroad. At home. Right here.

–   No one is safe.

–   I tried to pull him off. But this man was frenzied. He'd lost his mind. He was overcome with anger and he poured it into the poor broken body of our dear colleague.

–   The attacker was captured by the authorities. We would like to kill him. But we need witnesses.

–   One of you must have been here yesterday. One of you must have just sat there, there, while, while –

–   Sorry to be heavy. Sorry.

–   Of course ninety-nine point nine per cent of the time life is wonderful. Life is great. Life is fabulous. Babies are born. I should know. I've got one.

–   The sun shines.

–   The sun shines and then you sleep in your bed for eight lovely hours next to the man or woman you love.

–   Or both if you are a bohemian.

–   Or both if you are a bohemian. And in the morning there is the smell of croissants as the girl takes them out of the oven.

–   And the children come bouncing on your bed calling 'Mummy! Daddy!'

—   Because children love the world.

—   As we all do.

—   We all do. We all love the world.

—   If only that tiny little point of the population would use the helplines to report incidents and and and –

—   One of you saw yesterday's incident.

—   One of you saw yesterday's incident and is not coming forward.

—   You're not coming forward. And what are you?

—   A rotten egg.

—   You are a filthy – thank you – rotten . . . And you're stinking, stinking, stinking –

—   Stinking out the whole bloody barrel, you, you, you –

—   But we'll, there's something we'll –

—   There is something we can do.

—   We can, we will act against the rotten egg who is not coming forward.

—   We can. We will. This is what we . . .

—   Since yesterday, a commission, a panel, a meeting of minds has been looking into this problem.

—   The problem of the rotten egg. Their chairman reports:

—   A range of options to punish the rotten eggs in a democratic and humane society. And after questioning witnesses and balancing investment and projected incomes, we have concluded that branding is the way forward.

—   Branding is the way forward.

—   Branding with a hot iron is the way forward.

—   So . . . we are seeking the right to brand those who do not report such incidents – with an iron. A bill is being drawn up to go before our elected –

—   Exactly, thank you. There will be branding with an iron. One of you will be —

—   It's an entirely natural process.

—   The iron will be heated to 250 degrees centigrade and you will be branded.

—   Just here [*above the right elbow*]. A livid scar will remain for life.

—   And why not? Why not? Why not? Why do you think you should get away with it? Well, you won't, this way you won't.

—   This way you go to a beach or a cocktail party or a — you sit in the foyer out there drinking your coffee and eating your breakfast roll and you *will* be recognisable to the rest of us.

—   'There goes a rotten egg.'

—   There goes a — I want to vomit —

—   There goes an — want to kick the cunt — ah oh, tee tee ee en ee gee gee —

—   It is necessary to do these things if we are to live in a civilised society.

—   A society where rights are matched by responsibilities.

—   I'm sure you, as a decent citizen, will join us in welcoming the branding of those who do not come forward. So come forward now — step out of the crowd and come forward now.

Pause.

—   Branding will hurt. We won't pretend . . .

—   You will be a pariah for — ooh — decades —

—   But listen, listen, there'll be forgiveness.

—   Somewhere.

—   There's always kind, liberal, kind, forgiving, liberal, kind people who will forgive.

—   There's always refuge from the mob.

- There's kindness in the world. There's always liberals.

- We even fund the liberals (*laughs*) to a small degree.

- In the report, a third of the study group actually – oh, bit of a surprise – thanked us for the branding.

- So come on, come on, lone sad, lonely sad man or woman, woman or man, step forward and report yesterday's incident.

- Step forward now.

Pause.

- No?

- No?

- No.

- Very well. (*A picture.*) Here's the member of our staff who is this morning critically ill following yesterday's assault. A rib has punctured his lung. There's bleeding in his brain.

- He's a an actor – yes. But he's a person. Above all else he is a person.

- And like any normal person he has a family.

- Can't you feel anything . . . ? Empathy . . . maybe?

- A normal guy with a mortgage and a wife. Just like normal guys everywhere.

- Good. Good. Good. Starting to feel his pain.

- Here's a message from his wife. Here's a message written from his bedside by his wife.

- Will you read it to us?

- Would you like me to?

- I certainly would.

- Then I shall: 'Please punish anyone who witnessed and did not report this terrible assault upon my husband. He is my rock. I have been married to him for twenty years and in all that time he has been a rock. He has never done anything but

good in this world. He loves life and treasures everything about
the freedom and democracy we enjoy. This morning, as I
brought him a cup of coffee, to his bedside, he held out his
hand to me and said the words: "I love you." This is my hope.
In all the middle of so much evil, love will always continue.
I know I've spoken to my elected representative and asked her
to ensure the new branding measure is passed without delay
and I hope anyone listening to this will do the same. Freedom
must triumph. Democracy must triumph. I want these rotten
eggs branded. I say it on my website, I'm blogging it to the
world, and please read it out to this morning's audience at
breakfast: brand them, brand them, brand them.'

—   A very clear voice.

—   An admirably clear voice.

—   It's the voice of the people and it's righteously raised in
anger.

—   (*Punches air.*) Hurrah!

—   (*Punches air.*) Hurrah!

—   (*Punches air.*) Hurrah!

News arrives.

—   And listen, I'm hearing . . . reports are coming in . . . ah.
Our elected representatives are meeting. A special meeting of
the House of Representatives has been called in the light of
yesterday's attack. The meeting has just begun . . . the debate
has started. The engine of democracy has swung into action.

—   Will a bill be introduced to allow branding to take place?

—   Oh, we're confident of that. It's the will of the people.

—   Will the branding be in public?

—   Will we carry it on prime time? There's an advertising
lobby for −

—   Will it be a ticketed event? The Culture Minister says −

—   Will medical and legal supervision be thorough?

– Or even excessive?

– Or even excessive.

– Or maybe the liberals will, maybe they'll chip away with their 'amendments'.

– As is their right.

– As is their right. In a democracy.

– Let's wait and see, shall we? Let's wait and see. But democracy is taking its course.

– Democracy and freedom and hope and truth.

– Can I ask that we say a prayer? A prayer – doesn't matter if you're not religious – can I ask that we say a prayer? A prayer that the voice of the people be heard in the House of our Elected Representatives.

– Well – why not?

– Why not?

– Why not?

– Why not?

They kneel.

– O Lord, we thank you for your normal world. We thank you for the normal men and normal women who move about this normal city. We thank you for the normal cultural and normal leisure activities we enjoy on this normal day.

– Blessed be the normal coffee we drink.

– Blessed be the normal breakfast roll we break and enjoy this morning.

– And blessed be Vermeer and Monteverdi, the jugglers and the comedians, the *Bacchae* of Euripides and the brilliant new plays that inhabit thy earth.

– Give us this day an excellent rate of interest.

– Blessed be this loyalty card.

–   In mall and in retail outlet, online and instore.

–   And cursed be the rotten eggs, those who witness the attacks and do not come forward.

–   Curse them as you once cursed Lucifer and the rebel army as you threw them into Hell.

–   O Lord, send wisdom to our elected representatives.

–   Send our elected representatives the wisdom to pass this legislation.

–   This legislation which will allow us to brand the rotten eggs.

–   Brand them.

–   Brand them forever.

–   Brand them forever and evermore.

–   Amen.

–   (*Punches air.*) Hallelujah! Amen!

–   It will come, it must come, that day must surely come. Then there will be fireworks and music and dancing and champagne. And oh, how happy our world will be.

–   A blessed place. A good place. A calm place. A happy place.

–   It's so close. It's just a, a, a –

–   A breath.

–   Yes. It's just a breath away.

A piece of new information arrives.

–   Excuse me, excuse me, excuse, could I . . .

–   We hope that you've planned a day of relaxing activities.

–   I know I have. I've planned a day of incredibly soothing activities.

–   It's a wonderful city. It's bristling with culture. There's comedy and opera and jugglers and – ooh – oratoria. And we should – what's the . . . ? – revel! We should revel in that.

—   Sorry. Sorry. Sorry. Bad bad bad bad tragic bad bad news. We have just heard that – sorry to say – that woman's husband, our colleague the actor, has just died.

—   Really?

—   Really. His internal injuries. Very severe internal injuries. Injuries sustained during the assault yesterday in this space. The assault for which as yet no witness has come forward.

—   I'm incredibly saddened by the unnecessary death of a fellow human being.

—   I am almost inconsolable. I'm sorry, I can't, a moment . . . I . . . oh my Lord. (*Sobs.*)

—   What is it? Come on, come on.

—   I spent – one summer – I never told anyone, but one summer . . .

—   Yes?

—   We were lovers that summer. Before his wife . . . We spent the summer on a boat drifting across a lake making love under the moon and stars. We read Shakespeare. *The Winter's Tale.* It was so beautiful. We had such a bond. Oh, this is hurting me very very very very deeply. Medication, counselling, what do I do?

—   A life lost.

—   Words cannot express the grief that any of us feel for that man's death.

—   Well – I'm feeling anger. I'm feeling the most incredible anger.

—   Then let it out.

—   Yes. Let it out. Give voice, give voice, give voice.

—   What sort of world is this? Really? What sort of world? We've been silent too long. We've kept our peace while the society, while the . . . while elements, the scum, the cancer, the evil scumming cancer dregs have had things their way. They've stomped all over us.

– Too right.

– Too right.

– Well, I for one have had enough. I've had enough. I want violence. I want attacks. I want the crushing hand. Don't tell me we can counsel them or give them money – we've tried that, I've tried that. I really believed . . . God, to think I really believed . . . But now is the time to strike them, strike them, strike them.

– Yes.

– Yes.

– I'm not going to be inhuman. I'm not going to gas them. But I will lock them all away forever. Into the darkness, all of you – go. Go. And let the normal people continue on their way. Sorry. Sorry.

– Please, don't. You were speaking for me.

– You were speaking for so many of us here.

– Yes?

– It's good to remind ourselves there are just a few rotten eggs.

– Stinking out the barrel.

– Please, we have to brand people. We have to. It's the only option. It's the only option under the circumstances. Who is your representative? Who are they? Will you be calling them, texting them, emailing them – today? Do it today you must, you must, you must, you must, you must.

– Democracy is there for you to make use of.

– Make use of democracy. Let's hear what the backbone has to say.

– We may lose it, we may lose it. Don't take it for granted. If you don't text or email now and call out for branding, democracy may wither away.

– Just wither away.

— And die. Democracy will be dead.

— It's up to you. Do you love democracy? Or do you hate democracy? Which is it going to be? Contact your representative now. Just text the words **BRAND THEM** now.

More information arrives.

— Just a moment while I . . .

— The city offers a full range of sporting, leisure, shopping and artistic facilities.

— It's wonderful. It's a range we're very proud of.

— Justifiably proud.

— Justifiably proud of. I'm planning a cycle ride, buying a juicer and listening to Monteverdi. What about you?

   I shall be ambling.

— Really?

— Oh yes, ambling with an itchy credit card and a rumbling tummy.

— Sounds good to me.

— Sounds brilliant to me. Hah hah. Utterly brilliant.

— A further message from Marion.

— Marion?

— From her husband's — now dead husband's — bedside. Marion, now a widow, sent us this message.

— 'Fuck the bastards. Fuck them. Fuck them. Round them up. Round them all up and take them up to the castle and tie them to a stake and burn them, burn them, burn them. Fuck.'

— I support you, Marion.

— I'm feeling what you're feeling and you're speaking for me.

— Marion adds: 'Please help the authorities. Please put pressure on your elected representatives. Let none of us sleep till we've beaten down every last door and burnt every last piece of scum flesh.'

—   Ah yes.

—   Ah yes.

—   The eloquence of the ordinary man or woman when impelled to act is incredible.

—   We're all incredible, wonderful people, apart from the rotten eggs.

—   And let's not forget that. Let's not forget to celebrate the wonderful, ordinary men and women.

—   The backbone. The backbone should be celebrated.

—   I know I'm celebrating it.

—   We're all celebrating it. We're all celebrating it. We're celebrating the men and women who get up in the morning, get up, drink their coffee for breakfast, then do their bit – do their bit to generate wealth for the ordinary families that make up this society. And tonight those families will be sitting down and sharing some lovely meals together after another normal day. I'm celebrating everything the backbone does.

—   So I'm asking you. Come forward now or be branded. Any witness – come forward. Now.

Long pause.

—   Nobody?

—   Nobody?

—   Nobody?

—   Nobody. Very well, very well, well, the search goes on. Thank you for your time. But one of you is the rotten egg. And we'll find you.

—   We'll find you and we'll brand you hard.

—   Sorry to be heavy. Sorry.

–   Of course ninety-nine point nine per cent of the time life
is wonderful. Life is great. Life is fabulous. Babies are born.
I should know. I've got one.

–   The sun shines. For instance, yesterday. Yesterday I was at
a garden centre. I drove out to a garden centre. And I watched
a couple – a man and woman in their thirties and a little boy
of about seven – and that couple chose a bench for their
garden. Nothing special. An ordinary couple, an ordinary
bench. But I was moved. I was very moved by the, the, the . . .
moved by the ordinariness of it, you see? Those are the people
we don't . . . we don't read about them in the papers. Just
the ordinary . . . not thugs, not terrorists, not scum . . . just
ordinary . . . and we should hear about them more. Let's hear
about them more.

–   After all, it's what most of us . . . We are mostly totally
normal.

–   And hooray for that.

–   Hooray.

–   One of you here must have witnessed last week's incident.

–   There must be a witness.

–   A man is dead.

–   We now know that there is a dead man and an ordinary
woman who has lost her rock. Who's coming forward?

–   Which of you saw the attack?

–   Come forward.

–   Come forward. Now.

–   Come forward.

–   Come forward now. Now. Now. Now.

Pause.

–   No? No?

–   No.

News arrives.

– Hang on, I'm getting a . . .

– Me too . . . Oh that is good news.

– That is excellent news.

– A recommendation from the commission. While finding the facts, while asking the questions that matter, the commission decided that –

– And I quote: 'There is a key problem. Your audience is not being monitored closely enough. Would you let these people walk down a street unobserved? Would you let them shop without following and recording? Then why oh why in the name of freedom and democracy are they sitting there unmonitored in the theatre?'

– So . . . we're installed cameras. In this space. We are installing microcameras in this space.

– There are CCTV cameras watching you at the moment.

– There are no . . . None of these cameras is a dummy camera. Every one of these is a real camera. A very real camera. And it will assist us to identify those who witnessed the assault and are failing to come forward.

– It was the most cost-effective . . .

– Under the circumstances. How will this work? How will we use this . . . ? Can you explain the . . . ?

– Certainly. Yes, certainly. We have a team of behavioural psychologists, that is to say a team trained in the psychology of behaviour, who are at the moment behind this wall analysing you for any signs of guilt. Any guilt will be evident in your behaviour and will be made known to us. There will be a dossier on each and every one of you here today and over the next twelve hours we'll be doing an extensive, objective, analytical analysis of each of you.

– We will identify the innocent. We will identify the guilty. The good. The evil.

– The backbone. And the rotten egg.

–   Can we just say . . . ? I'd like to say on behalf of all . . .
Just say . . . Sorry for any inconvenience this may cause.

–   Sorry.

–   But really, for the innocent what possible inconvenience
could this cause?

–   Well, indeed.

–   Indeed.

–   If I was an innocent person – as I am – would I object to a
simple observation by a fully trained behavioural psychologist?
Would I object? Would I? I put the question.

–   Well, clearly . . . no.

–   Clearly not.

–   I would visit garden centres. I would wake to the smell of
coffee and croissants prepared by the girl and I would say to
my beautiful wife: 'I think a visit to the garden centre this
morning.' Would I mind if a camera was watching? Would
I object to observation and analysis?

–   Clearly not.

–   Clearly not. I would have a camera in my car, a camera
in the petrol station, a camera in the quiet corner where I
chose my garden bench. And I would have them there happily,
I would . . . I would . . .

–   Embrace – ?

–   Embrace them. Because here in my heart of hearts, here in
my soul, in my gut, in my head, I am clean, I am clean, I am
pure, I am pure, oh I am sweet and pure.

–   As are we all.

–   As are we all apart from the scum.

–   The scum.

–   The scum.

–   The scum.

– We'll watch and identify and crush and we'll, oh how we'll, the time is coming, it's coming now, when the scum will be wiped away and only the backbone will be left.

– Hallelujah!

– Hallelujah!

– Hallelujah!

– O Lord O Lord O my God my Father my God thy world will be cleansed. It shall, it shall, it shall. Just as thy Heaven was made free from the sinful ones, just as you cast Lucifer down, so shall our city, our country, our empire be clean, clean, clean, clean.

– Please don't let the cameras bother you. Act normally. Smile or frown or . . . cry. Yes, you can cry if you want to. Sob. Whatever you feel is appropriate. But in no way should you let the cameras bother you.

– Why would you?

– Why would you?

News arrives.

– Excuse me, I'm getting a . . . something . . .

– Yesterday I walked by the river. It was a beautiful day. I watched some planes overhead. Some of our brave boys and girls practising for the new surge, and I thought: this is perfect, this is lovely, this is the most perfect day of my life. And I ate linguine in the evening.

– Oh yes! Yes! Yes! It's been passed. It's gone through on a fair majority. The bill has been passed.

– Oh that is good news. O my God, O my God, O my God.

– That's marvellous. That is – oh yes!

– That is fan-fucking-tastic. That is . . .

– Democracy and truth democracy and truth democracy and truth democracy and truth democracy and truth democracy and truth democracy and truth democracy and truth.

– Fireworks and champagne.

– Champagne and fireworks.

– Handel, speak for us. Handel, give us thy spirit as we celebrate this moment of history.

– A dance a dance a dance.

Handel is played as they dance and punch the air.

– Hurrah for the normal, the normal, the normal.

Dancing ends.

– We can now brand anyone who witnessed yesterday's incident but does not come forward. Under medical and legal supervision, an iron heated to an exact temperature of 250 degrees centigrade, will be applied to the right arm just here until a permanent mark is left.

Information arrives.

– We're getting a . . .

– My faith is restored . . . sometimes you think . . . you think . . . democracy is failing . . . you think – I don't know – it's not working . . . Why this vote, this cross on this box? Why? Sometimes you can't . . . until something comes along, something, and hope is, trust and hope and – God bless democracy – hope and trust are reborn.

– There have been some amendments.

– Oh. The liberals.

– Oh.

– Some amendments were made during the passing of the bill in the interests of a humane society.

– As we surely are.

– We surely are.

– The branding will take place privately. TV crews and ticket holders will not be admitted as had been earlier proposed. And calls for burning at the stake at the castle have been, as they say, 'kicked into the long grass', where they will be considered by a committee.

—   Oh well, still . . . a victory for democracy and humanity.

—   Democracy and humanity.

—   Democracy and humanity. Our core values. Once again they shine through in every act of our enlightened society.

—   Marion, the grieving widow, has welcomed the new measures while questioning if they go far enough.

—   'I want them burnt at the stake. I really do. I want to see them scream as the flames encase their fetid bodies and I want to spit on their ashes as they are swept away. I will be campaigning tirelessly for burning at the stake. Join me at my website and let's make the voice of ordinary men and women heard.'

News arrives.

It is understood that the first brandings are now taking place in a government-recognised but privately owned centre near here. It is private event. There is medical and legal supervision. No tickets have been sold. No TV crews are present.

—   So different from our enemies. In our enemies' countries, people are dragged kicking and screaming into public places and they are branded without proper medical or legal supervision.

—   Revolting.

—   My stomach is turning.

—   Turning. There – in the heart of that evil empire – people are burnt frequently at the stake.

—   Ugh.

—   Ugh.

—   Their only crime? Their only crime? What is their only crime? Their only crime –

—   It's . . .

– Oh yes.

– Their only crime to stand up and say: 'I am a person. I am my own distinct person. I have my own personality and my own thoughts.' And for this, these people are burnt.

– Disgusting.

– Disgusting.

– Disgusting.

– How they yearn for freedom and light and choice, democratic choice, for rights and responsibilities.

– How they yearn, and how we, many of them, take them for granted.

– This is your last chance. Marion is grieving. Her husband is dead. Yesterday's incident was brutal.

– Come forward now or be branded. Any witness – come forward. Now.

Long pause.

– Nobody?

– Nobody?

– Nobody?

– Nobody.

– I'm getting some. We . . .

– The tapes of today's meetings will be analysed.

– Our behavioural psychologists will identify the guilty.

– Your branding will take place before nightfall.

– We're being joined by . . . BRING HIM IN! BRING HIM IN!

*A **Man** is dragged in by two **Guards**/front-of-house staff. He is very weak.*

– A historical moment.

– This is history.

–   This is the first person – correction – the first rotten egg to be branded since the passing of the new legislation. He has been brought straight to us from the branding centre. He has come because he wishes to speak to you. He has words. Well, my friend, now is your moment, now is the moment, now is your time so . . . speak.

Man (*weakly*)   I am a rotten egg. I know that now. I see that now. The mark is here on my arm for all of you to see. Like a broken wing. Please despise me, please hate me. That is your right – and your responsibility. How I wish I could lead a normal life. Paint watercolours. Go fly fishing. Teach my daughter Spanish. Talk online with my friend in Southern Australia. But this will never happen. I am evil and I have been banished from Paradise forever. This is justice and I embrace it. I did not come forward. I witnessed a violent incident in the New Town and yet I did not come forward. Why didn't I . . . ? For one reason and one reason alone. I am a bad person. There is no point trying to understand me. There is no point giving me money. I am bad bad bad bad bad. Please assist the authorities. Please report violent incidents. Please come forward. God bless the cameras. God bless our elected representatives. Democracy and truth and history and freedom and . . .

He loses consciousness.

–   This city is a lovely place.

–   I think so. I think it's lovely.

–   I may look at some Vermeer, there's a folk band promised in the park and I'm looking forward to Monteverdi enormously.

–   Do you know what I'm going to do? What I'm going to do right now? Right now I'm going to have a great cup of coffee.

–   Oh yes. For most of us it's going to be a fabulous day.

–   What a great world it is. Good morning.

The **Speakers** *leave. The* **Man** *remains unconscious on the floor.*

Play Seven

Crime and Punishment

A **Soldier,** *a* **Woman.**

Soldier Interview begins 9.32 a.m. (*To* **Woman.**) State your name.

Woman . . .

Soldier 9.32 a.m. State your name.

Woman . . .

Soldier Refusal to state name. You speak English? Do you speak English? Do you speak English? Do you speak English? Speak English. Speak English.

Woman Speak English.

Soldier English is spoken. Are you comfortable? Are you comfortable? Are you comfortable?

He raises his gun.

Woman I am comfortable.

Soldier Subject is comfortable. 9.33 a.m. I'm talking . . . talking to . . . ? [*State your name.*]

Woman . . .

He raises his gun.

Woman A woman who was once a wife and mother and is now a widow.

Soldier You are comfortable? You have been given coffee and a bread roll. You have received medication. You are feeling tranquil?

Woman I am comfortable.

Soldier And almost tranquil. Well, that is good news. That's very good news. Tell me about the dictator.

Woman He was a very bad man.

Soldier   Of course he was.

Woman   My husband was not allowed to teach. His post was removed from the university. My brother had a hot iron applied to his arm because he wrote in a newspaper.

Soldier   So . . . a very bad man.

Woman   A very bad man.

Soldier   A very bad man.

Woman   But a strong man. Maybe sometimes a country needs a strong, bad man. This is what we debate late into the night: was it better for our poor country to have a bad man but no civil war? So much argument. I think you say frying pan or fire. But I say: in our world, there is a Hell with a Devil in it, below that another Hell with another Devil in it and below that another Hell with another Devil. There are only Hells and we are angels with broken wings and we are all burning in these Hells and which one do we choose?

Soldier   Your mouth is pornographic.

Woman   I'm sorry.

Soldier   I find your mouth has something . . .

Woman   I'm sorry. This is a time for grief for me.

Soldier   I've fought my way through the desert. My tranquillisers were lost. My girl texted to say she's got together with this – sorry – fuckwit. I mean, what's this all about? What is this all about?

Woman   Please, can I go? My mother-in-law is very bad. The shelling, she needs me. I want to –

Soldier   No no no. You sit, you sit, you sit. 9.34 a.m. Interview continues. Describe the day the statue comes down.

Woman   Please, I am worried. My mother-in-law may die. I feel grief.

Soldier   And my, what about my . . . ? We all have . . . The statue comes down.

Woman (*flatly*)   The troops have arrived in the city. My husband and son have died in the bombing. I am told that my mother-in-law is in the hospital. Very critical in the shelling. I am trying to get to the hospital. It is very hard. Troops and insurgents. Many of the roads are blocked. A soldier comes to me: 'Want to be on TV? Want to be on TV?' 'Please, I must find the hospital.' 'Come on, you're a pretty girl, be on TV.' Soldier pushes me with gun into square. Two hundred people have been chosen to go into square. 'You passed the audition,' laughs woman next to me and many people laugh. Maybe this is funny. I'm sorry, I did not find this funny. Soldiers have attached wires and wires to truck to great statue of dictator. There is a rock band. They sing Elton John and Freddie Mercury. I don't believe they are homosexuals. 'I must go to the hospital. I must see my mother-in-law.' Soldier blocks me. 'Square is closed off now. This is freedom. This is democracy. This is history. Stay.' I am pushed back into crowd by soldier's gun. There are many TV crews. We wait for a long time. My mind is so upset. I think my mother-in-law may die and think I never came to her. 'What are we waiting for?' I ask woman in crowd. 'For prime time,' she says. Is this a religious belief?

Soldier   No.

Woman   What is . . . ?

Soldier   It's TV. It's ratings. It's advertisers.

Woman   Thank you. I've wondered. Finally prime time comes – there is a green light to signify the prime time has begun – and the statue comes down.

Soldier   And how did you feel?

Woman   Nothing.

Soldier   Freedom. Democracy. History.

Woman   Yes, we used to talk about those things when my husband lost his job at the university, but actually . . .

Soldier   You're an incredible woman.

Woman   I don't feel anything for these big words.

Soldier   Do you love me?

Woman   I'm sorry?

Soldier   I really want you to love me.

Woman   I've been a widow for five days. Your army . . .

Soldier   I'm in a lot of pain here. I want you to love me. How do I make you fall in love with me?

Woman   My duty is with my mother-in-law.

Soldier   If we were back home, I'd take you to a bar, drink all you can, a film, a Chinese, I'd make love to you very gently. I'd know what to do. But here – how do I make love to you here?

Woman   My husband was laid to rest yesterday. My son will be laid to rest tomorrow.

Soldier   Frigid bitch.

Woman   Please.

Soldier   Sorry, sorry but . . . look at me, I'm a person, I'm a human person, with a heart, I have so much love to give.

Woman   I have a right to respect.

Soldier   I am opening my heart to you and what am I getting?

Woman   I understand that I am being held in the occupied zone but still the international treaties give me the right to respect.

Soldier   Oh yada oh yada / oh yada oh yada dooo.

Woman   If you do not give me that respect, I demand the right –

Soldier   Fuck this, fuck this, fuck. You wrote letters, I bet you, articles all during the dictator years?

Woman   My husband –

Soldier   Exactly, exactly.

Woman   We campaigned.

Soldier   And you were published in the – yes – there was newspaper stuff in my paper? TV documentary crews . . . hidden cameras . . . blah blah.

Woman   The world had to know.

Soldier   Cruel life under the dictator. Freedom. Democracy. You shouted it out? You shouted it out? You shouted it?

Woman   I campaigned.

Soldier   Well, we're here now. History is happening. Freedom. Democracy is happening. Happening. And you won't even – frigid bitch. You don't even feel a little bit of love?

Woman   Thank you.

Soldier   I'm sorry?

Woman (*flatly*)   Thank you for freeing my country. We suffered greatly. We prayed for freedom and democracy. You were brave. You fought your way through the desert. You pulled down the dictator's statue. You made history. You have given us Freedom. Democracy is happening. (*Gets up.*) Now my mother-in-law –

Soldier   Oh no, oh no, oh. 9.39. Interview continues.

Woman   What do you want?

Soldier   Don't play with me.

Woman   According to the protocols –

Soldier   Don't use that stuff on me.

Woman   I am now being held against all the international agreements.

Soldier   The heart is so much bigger. The human heart than any –

Woman   This should be recorded as an illegal –

Soldier   For love, for love. I want you to understand. Don't you understand how hurt I am? How much I need love?

Woman   My husband died easily – a bullet in his head.

Soldier   Every moment you don't love me you're torturing me.

Woman   My son was slower. His spine was crushed by a bomb. There was a pneumonia in the hospital. It was many days.

Soldier   Is there no woman – no woman who can ever just give me the love that I deserve?

Woman   I look around at the city. I look at you now. And I think this is all a dream. Nightmare. I'm walking in peace somewhere else. But this is grief. Everything around me is real. Everything around me is happening. Only I don't feel like this is real because of grief. One day everything will become real again.

Soldier   If you love.

Woman   There will come a day when the numbing is over.

Soldier   Or maybe never, maybe, you know, maybe, maybe . . . my mum . . . cancer blah blah blah   I was ten . . . she smoked forty a day so what can you . . . ? But nothing's been real since . . . that bitch fucked off . . . I'm a kid and the bitch fucks off . . .

Woman   Show some respect.

Soldier   She'd have smoked in the fucking coffin if she could . . . She goes . . . she goes . . . We sit by her side till five in the morning and then she goes . . . And nothing is real again. We got a 'happy family'. My dad meets Marion in the garden centre a couple of years later. We're happy. But I want something . . .

Woman   Your mother is resting.

Soldier   But me. But me. Don't want to be – but me? I am walking this earth and still there's nothing. It's all numbness. Nothing's real. Come on. Help me here. Help me. Hold me. Tell me that you love me.

Woman   There is nothing in the international agreements –

Soldier   Oh please – paper, talks – we're people, we're people –

Woman   This interview must be conducted according to protocol.

Soldier   Bitch bitch bitch bitch bitch bitch bitch bitch.

Woman   You could be my son. I would smack him.

Soldier   I could be the man you love.

Woman   I stole the medicine for my son from another child's bed. In war you will do anything. But still my child died. Both children died.

Soldier   I saw you on the TV when the statue came down. We'd occupied the hotel. Found some beer. Turned on the TV. Saw your face and I thought: 'There is something about her, there's something . . . she's got . . . ' And so when I saw you I said, 'Okay, pull her in. I can question her.' You see? You see? But it was stupid. Enjoy the moment. But you're not loving me back so – I can't carry on, just can't. A life without love is . . . I'm going to . . . 9.41 a.m. I have decided that life on this planet is pointless. There is no love in this world. I have decided to shoot my brains out. There will now be the sound of gunfire.

Woman   No.

Soldier   Stand back, please. I don't know what happens. But I guess – mess.

Woman   No.

Soldier   Maybe it's enough to have seen the most beautiful, wonderful woman. Maybe that's enough. Maybe to ask for her love back is too much. Maybe I'm asking for too much.

Woman   Don't be a child. Put the gun away. NO.

Soldier   You gonna hold me?

Woman   I'm gonna hold you.

Soldier   Oh thank you thank you thank you.

She holds him. A pietà: mother and child.

My life has been . . . I bring you Freedom and Democracy.
And now you bring me love.

Woman   I am holding you.

Soldier   9.42 a.m. Operation Enlightenment is complete.
I am being held in the arms of a woman who feels love for me.

Woman   I am a mother and wife who is grieving. My
mother-in-law is in the hospital.

Soldier   We are each of us broken people but if we reach
out and offer another person love we're . . . That is the future.

Woman   How can I feel love?

Soldier   Of course you feel love.

Woman   It wouldn't be right for me to feel that now.

Soldier   Forget about right. Forget about wrong.

Woman   I am unable to feel that now.

Soldier   So you're saying . . . you're saying?

Woman   Please, I'm holding you. That is enough. That
should be enough.

Soldier   I want more. Please. I want more.

Woman   That is enough.

Soldier   Oh no.

Woman   Shhh now, shhh. Rest in my arms.

Soldier   My country is safe. It's a safe, numb place. The
people are happy people. Underneath I ache but still I . . .
I can go to the supermarket, I can go to the garden centre,
I go for a cup of coffee. It's alright. Why did I leave that? Shat
my pants fighting in the desert. Saw a man have his head
blown off right beside me and that was it – shit in my pants.
Did all that because you were crying out for freedom and
democracy but now, but now . . . I need to be loved, okay? Is
that so wrong, okay? Is that so fucking wrong? And I tell you
this, I tell you this –

Woman   Calm yourself.

Soldier   No. I will invade every fucking country in the fucking world, okay? I will fucking invade them all. Got the will, got the firepower and I will fucking do it. They want supermarkets, they want garden centres, they want Xboxes, they want Starbucks. They got it. It's coming. It's coming. It's fucking coming.

Woman   I'm going now.

Soldier   No you don't, bitch, no you don't.

Woman   My mother-in-law –

Soldier   Fuck her fuck her fuck her.

Woman   – will need me . . .

Soldier *fires.*

Soldier   9.43 a.m. I have shot detainee in the foot to prevent her escape.

Woman   Oh – bastard.

Soldier   Everything is coming to the whole fucking world. See me? I'm bigger than mountains and rivers and seas. My head is big, my arms are big, my dick is big, my feet are big. They are big enough to go anywhere.

Woman   Take me to the hospital.

Soldier   I will go everywhere. Freedom and Democracy will be everywhere. And somewhere, somewhere, somewhere, somewhere someone will say to me: 'I love you.' Is that too much to ask? Is it that someone should see through all the shit – the shelling, the mortar fire, the landmines, blah – and just see I'm a person looking for love?

Woman   I demand to be taken to the hospital under protocol –

Soldier   Shut the fuck up.

He fires.

9.43 a.m. I have shot detainee's right kneecap because she, because . . . there was a provocation. You okay?

Woman   There's great pain.

Soldier   I suppose, yes . . . Detainee reporting pain. Some blood but not to an excessive degree. Do you love me?

Woman   Please − the hospital.

Soldier   Do you love me?

Woman   I have to be seen by a doctor.

Soldier   It won't kill you. Do you love me?

Woman   Take me to the hospital.

Soldier   Say you love me.

Woman   I love you.

Soldier   Do you mean that?

Woman   Oh please. I love you I love you I love love you I love you I love you I love love you.

Soldier   Do you mean that? Look me in the eyes and say it. I have to see you . . . Look me in the eyes. Here.

Holds her head so their eyes meet.

If you can't say it to my eyes it doesn't count.

Woman   . . .

Soldier   Well?

Woman   . . .

Soldier   Well?

Woman   . . .

Soldier   There's nothing there. Fuck. You're dead. You're . . .

Woman   I am feeling so much pain.

Soldier   Love me. Love me. Love me. Love me. Be my mum. Be my girl. Be . . . just . . . I don't . . . you can . . . any . . . shit . . . be . . .

Woman   Oh.

Soldier   9.44 a.m. Detainee has lost consciousness. I have
impure thoughts. I have thoughts of rape and torture. I want
to abuse my position and abuse this woman. I am reporting
what I am feeling. But I am not driven by animal desire. I am
a human being and like all human beings I have a choice.
Rape and torture are only appropriate when dealing with terror
suspects and only with proper medical and legal supervision. I
do not give myself permission to rape and torture the detainee.
I choose, as a human being, not to rape, torture or abuse the
detainee. Bless Freedom. Bless Democracy. The right choices
have been made. Suspect is regaining consciousness. You
alright? You alright? You alright?

Woman   Please?

Soldier   I am the man you love.

Woman   I want to get away from here.

Soldier   I'd earn lots of money. I'd buy you so much stuff.
And at night if I was lonely and afraid you'd hold me. Isn't
that great? Doesn't that sound great? We'd watch TV. Eat
Chinese. Play the Xbox. Go to the garden centre. And we'd
make love together very slow and gentle and beautiful. I'd get
jealous of the love you give our kiddies but I'd get over it with
counselling and we'd be very happy together. There's nothing
like the love a woman feels for a man. It's incredible.

Woman   This is your freedom? This is your democracy?
How stupid we were. I cheered you through the desert. I called
out to you because . . . what a fool I've been. You are just
another hell.

Soldier   No. My country, it really is –

Woman   Fuck you.

Soldier   My country's a better place.

Woman   Fuck. May the ghost of my husband and my son
and a thousand million angry spirits rise up from the ground
and bring their hate to you. May the hospitals and the craters
and the battlefields throw up the angry dead and may they
find you and may they kill you. The spirit of an angry nation

will not rest until you are destroyed. Of this I am sure: your
country and your people and your civilisation will burn and
be thrown into the flames of Hell for the horror of this day.
We will never be together. I want freedom. I want democracy.
I don't want this. I don't want you. I want a better world but
how can I . . . ? Is every world just a hell? I will go to the
hospital.

Soldier   Please. Say: 'I love you.'

Woman   I don't do it.

Soldier   I'll cut out your tongue.

Woman   I don't do it.

Soldier   I'll cut it out.

Woman   I don't do it.

Soldier   Because you can't . . . Oh this is a pointless world
with no point and the . . . still in the . . . freedom, democracy,
freedom, democracy, freedom, democracy, freedom, democracy.

Woman   Hear me now. Look. In the eyes. Yes? I hate you
I hate you I hate you I hate you I –

He cuts out her tongue. She struggles and then passes out.

Soldier   9.47 a.m. I have cut out detainee's tongue. My
mission is pointless. Nobody loves me. Now I must choose if
I shoot out my brains. Maybe there is love in another place,
maybe if we invade again then a woman will say . . . or maybe
it is better to shoot now. I wish I had an order from a superior.
Please somebody tell me, 'Shoot out your brains' or, 'Son,
don't shoot out your brains.' But there is no order from above.
The choice is mine. This is democracy. This is what we call
democracy. Democracy – I hate you.

Play Eight

Love (But I Won't Do That)

Soldier, Marion.

Soldier I'm aching for a fuck.

Marion Don't.

Soldier You don't . . . women . . .

Marion I'm having more coffee. Would you like more coffee? I think maybe some more coffee.

Soldier Last night I really thought we might –

Marion This is Fairtrade, which is important, isn't it?

Soldier You could feel my hands on you, right? That wasn't really sleep?

Marion Even drinking a cup of coffee you can liberate or exploit –

Soldier My finger, you weren't actually sleeping through that?

Marion We must make sure we only deal with the coffee farms where the labourers are treated with dignity, where a minimum wage is –

Soldier You felt me, huh? Come on, you felt me? See this finger – these fingers – these fingers still smell of you so don't tell me? Don't tell me, huh? Huh?

Marion I'm a sound sleeper.

Soldier It's not a bad smell.

Marion I have camomile tea and a herb pillow. I'm right off.

Soldier You were pretending, you were pretending, come on, come on, just cos I'm in a uniform, just cos I carry a gun,

I'm not fucking thick. Don't treat me like I'm fucking stupid, okay? I AM NOT FUCKING STUPID.

Marion   I wish you wouldn't eat sugary snacks. Anger –

Soldier   AAAAGGGGGHHHHHHH!

Marion   So much anger is caused by sugary snacks.

Soldier   Anger anger anger anger is caused by –

Marion   The blood sugar shoots up and then slumps down, a roller coaster of –

Soldier   My dick. My balls. My cock's up for hours, you could see that –

Marion   I was preparing, cooking, making the linguine.

Soldier   All evening you knew.

Marion   I get very lost in handmade pasta. It does taste better.

Soldier   But still you and then you, you you faked sleep? Yes? Yes? Yes?

Marion   Let's not – I've got a busy day – you?

Soldier   You weren't asleep.

Marion   We've got the new boys from the viral marketing team coming in to brief us before the client arrives. Apparently eighty per cent of the spend of this one is going to be viral. Only twenty per cent on the more, on the, the, the older media.

Soldier   When am I going to get a fuck?

Marion   They think I'm a dinosaur, they really do. When I talk about targeting the spend on TV they just laugh in my face and call out 'Pterodactyl!'

Soldier   I've got to have a fuck.

Marion   I've started to play along. Flap my wings. Caw caw caw. Pterodactyl. Caw caw caw.

Soldier   We're supposed to be, this is supposed to be, this is an . . . alliance.

Marion   I'm supposed to be their boss, but it's important to show you can laugh, yes? And I can laugh, yes? Yes? Yes? Yes? Yes? (*Laughs, then cries.*) Oh I'm sorry, sorry.

Soldier   Hey.

Marion   No I am, I'm really, really . . . oh. (*Cries.*) I'm sorry.

Soldier   Don't . . . let it out.

Marion   There's just been so much to take on board, you know? Everything's moved . . . so fast. And I suppose there's bound to be stress, isn't there?

Soldier   Of course.

Marion   I've tried taking St John's wort and I think that does kind of –

Soldier *kisses* **Marion.**

Soldier   Was that alright?

Marion   Of course. That was lovely.

Soldier   So I'm not just an animal?

Marion   Of course not, no. You're a person.

Soldier   Sometimes you make me feel like an animal.

Marion   I don't mean to. Sorry. Sorry.

Soldier   I'm just here to defend you. The kids. The house. That's what I'm here for.

Marion   I know, and we're all very grateful.

Soldier   I like it here. Pleased when the CO picked out this house for me.

Marion   It's a lovely house.

Soldier   You're a lovely lady.

Marion   Thank you.

Soldier   And I'm . . . ? What do you think about me?

Marion   I think you're a big strong handsome brave soldier fighting for freedom and democracy, all that we believe in.

Soldier   So why . . . ?

Marion   And, if we didn't have you, our world would have ceased to exist long ago and been eaten up by the evil ones.

Soldier   You lock the bathroom door. A piss. A shit.

Marion   You don't want to –

Soldier   A shower. You lock the door. You keep me out . . .

Marion   Well . . .

Soldier   You change behind that door. You take off your day clothes and you come up in that huge great T-shirt –

Marion   It's comfortable.

Soldier   You pull the duvet up to your chin, you cling to the side of the bed –

Marion   I'm sorry.

Soldier   How many times have we made love?

Marion   It's only been three weeks.

Soldier   How many times?

Marion   I don't . . . I'm not counting.

Soldier   I'm counting. I'm counting every minute of every . . . I'm counting it out. Every last. Twice.

Marion   Yes?

Soldier   We've fucked twice.

Marion   I thought more . . .

Soldier   Not counting the failures. One of us has to come, okay? If neither comes then –

Marion   Can I put the bread away now or would you like more toast?

Soldier   Twice in three weeks, what would you call that? What would you say that is?

Marion   I'm going over to rye bread. There's bloating.

Soldier   I would say that is shit that is – that is – yes that is – okay – that is fucking shit, yeah?

Marion   I'm sorry.

Soldier   Allies. Bedfellows. Why are we doing all this unless we fuck?

Marion   I don't know.

Soldier   You've got to – How do I feel, how are you making me feel, have you thought – what do I – ?

Marion   I really don't –

Soldier   Rejected. Hurt. Belittled. Patronised. Humiliated. You lie with your duvet up, your T-shirt on and your – the legs are clamped and that's what you are doing to me –

Marion   That's not what I mean.

Soldier   You know exactly, exactly, exactly, you know exactly what you are doing.

Marion   I don't. NO. NO.

Soldier   Yes yes YES, you are hurting me – here inside – as though I have no feelings – but I have feelings – I have a huge – I have feelings – I – I – I –

Marion   Yes, of course. I'm sorry. I've been a selfish person. I've led a privileged life. I want to learn from you. I am learning from you. Please.

Soldier   I've got a girl back home.

Marion   You never said.

Soldier   Well, now we're . . .

Marion   Of course.

Soldier   She still texts me. I wanna marry her one day. But this is a long war.

Marion   One day.

Soldier   Evil always loses somehow but sometimes can't
see . . .

Marion   With guys like you fighting –

Soldier   Thanks.

Marion   I'm right behind you.

Soldier   Here's my girl. (*Photo on mobile phone.*) Bethany, she's
called.

Marion   She's very pretty.

Soldier   I know she's fat. She likes all the crap stuff. Cold
pizza for breakfast. She doesn't have a Stairmaster like you.

Marion   Everyone's different.

Soldier   But she likes a shag. Every night. Two or three
times on a Sunday.

Marion   Gosh.

Soldier   Imagine that – to grab hold of that any time you
want to. Really lose yourself in there.

Marion   I need to get the car out of the garage.

Soldier   That's what I'm used to, see? Fuck after fuck after
fuck.

Marion   We're going to have to move your stuff so I can get
the car out of the garage.

Soldier   When you're used to that much fucking –

Marion   I don't want to be late for the viral boys.

Soldier   And now you – it's physically, emotionally,
psychologically – there's a lot of hurt. Do you know that?

Marion   I understand.

Soldier   So do you think you can . . . ?

Marion   I'll do my best.

Soldier Tonight?

Marion I'll really try.

Soldier I want a really good session. And I want it tonight.

Marion Well, I'll see what I can do, okay?

Soldier No. Let's not 'see what you can do'. Let's promise.

Marion I need the car out of the garage.

Soldier I want a promise. Here. Now. I want you to promise that you will take off your clothes in front of me. No bathroom, no – I'll watch as you get totally, totally naked. You will play with your breasts for a moment, you will cup, you will run, you will trail over your nipples before you offer yourself to me –

Marion You've thought about this.

Soldier Three weeks. I will take you. You will not be passive. You will not get fucked. We will fuck together. Together we will fuck for a long time.

Marion I'm not Bethany.

Soldier I know that. She's – home. You're –

Marion I'm older. I'm different.

Soldier I want to come on your face tonight. That's what I really want. Pull out, climb over you and –

Marion No.

Soldier I'm sorry?

Marion No.

Soldier You're not going to . . . ?

Marion I don't like that. That's horrible. Some man –

Soldier Me –

Marion – coming on my face. It's too . . . I feel cheap. I'm not a tart. I want some dignity.

Soldier That's what I'm going to do.

Marion At least allow me some dignity, okay? I'm a person. I have money. I own a house. I have children in good schools. I own my company. Yes, we need you. Yes, there's a war on. Yes, you're protecting us. Yes yes yes, but for fuck's sake, for fuck's sake, for fuck's . . . give me a little . . . Cum dribbling down my . . . no, please.

Soldier If it's what I want to do.

Marion It's not what I want to do.

Soldier Well, I'm sorry I'm sorry I'm sorry –

Marion Now can we move your stuff so I can get my car out of –

Soldier I've been fucking lenient with this, I've played along with this, you know?

Marion I just have a massive thing about punctuality.

Soldier Well, let's not pretend, eh? No more fucking pretending? No more pretence. I am sick of this pretence.

Marion I really want your help.

Soldier The rules are changing, okay? Okay? If I say strip – you strip, no questions asked. If I say legs open, the legs open – no fucking about. If I say enjoy yourself, you will enjoy yourself. You will come and come and come and come like you have never come before.

Marion I can't.

Soldier You can. You will.

Marion No.

Soldier Oh yes.

Marion What are you? You're brutal, you're cruel, you're clumsy, you bring your boots through the house, your hands are huge and rough as sandpaper, you smell of cigarettes and beer, your erection against my back makes me sick, the smell of your shit in my bathroom lingers for hours –

Soldier All of this, all of this, all of this, all of this, all of this is true.

Marion   It's enough that I have you in the house, that I let you in my bed, but now you –

Soldier   I will do what I want.

Marion   You will take away every last piece of dignity from me.

Soldier   I will I will and you will love me for it and you will thank me for it.

Marion   No I won't do that fuck off no I won't won't no fuck off.

Soldier   Because I am bigger. I am stronger. I have guns. I have an army. I am everything. So if my spunk –

Marion   Please. I don't want to do it.

Soldier   – over your face makes you feel bad –

Marion   I'm grateful for all you – I respect –

Soldier   – you live with that, yes? You live with that.

Marion   I can't.

Soldier   You're sure?

Marion   I . . . Maybe my upbringing . . . some flaw . . . I never smoked with the other girls after lights out so maybe . . . maybe I'm uptight, but still . . . my fault . . . but no.

Soldier   Then this is what will happen. I will talk to my CO today. I will explain that I have been experiencing difficulties with cooperation. This ally wants everything her own fucking way –

Marion   All I –

Soldier   SHUT UP SHUT THE FUCK UP DID I GIVE YOU PERMISSION TO FUCKING SPEAK? NO. SO SHUT – I will explain and he will understand and we will withdraw from this house. I will take my weapons and my mines and my – and I will be reassigned, a house where they want me, a house where –

Marion   I'm sorry.

Soldier   A house where they're not too fucking stuck-up to get their fucking pussy wet.

Marion   No, I like that, it's just –

Soldier   And no defences, no weapons, no soldier, how long you gonna – ? How long you really gonna last before the insurgents . . . ? A couple of days, weeks if you're lucky, month'd be a miracle. You can't fight – your kids can't fight, so . . .

Marion   Don't go.

Soldier   All you can hope for is a good clean bomb to carry you off straight away, nothing too messy-

Marion   Stay, stay, stay, stay, stay, stay, stay –

Soldier   I'm sorry, you what? You what?

Marion   I'm begging you to stay.

Soldier   Say that again.

Marion   Please.

Soldier   This is another picture of Bethany. (*On phone.*) That's just after I've come over her face.

Marion   . . .

Soldier   How did you think Bethany looks with my cum over her face?

Marion   . . .

Soldier   I think she looks very beautiful.

Marion   Please. My meeting. I need you to escort me. Your gun is –

Soldier   You understand the terms? I'm staying on if . . .

Marion   Yes. I understand.

Soldier   And accept? We got to work together on this one.

Marion   I understand and I accept. You are very welcome here. Thank you for protecting us. Thank you for giving me your body.

Soldier   And my love. I've got love . . . I know in three weeks we can't . . . but in time . . . I only really knew Bethany after the first year.

Marion   You still love her?

Soldier   Always. But I'm here now. Am I brutal with you?

Marion   Sometimes you seem . . .

Soldier   I know I am. I don't mean to be. I suppose that's war. That's fighting. You don't notice. You get scared. And then you find yourself doing cruel things.

Marion   It was your regiment shot my husband.

Soldier   You can't always tell who's theirs and who's ours.

Marion   Is that why you asked for my house to protect?

Soldier   He died straight away. I'm a good shot. He was coming towards me. I took him out. He looked surprised, then he died – like that.

Marion   His face was still surprised in the morgue.

Soldier   I feel guilt.

Marion   I'm still waiting for my feelings.

Soldier   But you learn in training – friendly fire is an inevitable consequence of war.

Marion   We hadn't had sexual intercourse for years, that side had gone so . . .

Soldier   I'll be gentle with you.

Marion   Thank you.

Soldier   But I have to do it. That's what men . . .

Marion   Of course. I understand. What's in the boxes blocking the garage?

Soldier   Ammunition. Six extra crates arrived last night. You were in the shower.

Marion   Let's move the crates so I can get to the meeting.

Soldier   You missing your husband?

Marion   He was here every minute for twenty years. Now there's nothing. It's very strange. Everything feels wrong.

Soldier   Maybe if I loved you . . .

Marion   Yes.

Soldier   We're going to have to get used to each other cos this war's going on a long time. This is just the beginning.

Marion   I really have to go.

Soldier   Can I do a picture of you with cum on your face tonight?

Marion   I . . .

Soldier   You'll look so beautiful.

Marion   I won't. I'll look old and uncomfortable and . . .

Soldier   You're going to have to learn to trust me. Can you do that? If you want protecting . . .

Marion   I'll learn to do that,

Soldier   Good girl.

Marion   But tonight please start slowly. You can humiliate me later. But tonight – I don't want to feel like a tart tonight, alright?

Soldier   Alright.

Marion   Let's just forget the world and make love tonight – soldier boy.

Soldier   To attention, ma'am.

Marion (*laughs*)   So I see.

Soldier   It's gonna be a good night.

Marion   I'm sure.

Soldier   And in time . . . love –

Marion   Let's wait. Just you – yeah.

Play Nine

The Mikado

Alan, Peter.

Alan   Isn't this lovely?

Peter   Yes.

Alan   It's lovely and calm here. Lovely and calm. Don't you think this is lovely and calm?

Peter   It's lovely and calm.

Alan   Would you say this is a Japanese garden?

Peter   The bridge is certainly . . .

Alan   Oh yes.

Peter   A Japanese bridge . . . (*Sings.*) 'Three little maids from school are we − '

Alan   Hah hah. (*Sings.*) 'Come from the ladies' sem-in-ar-y − '

Peter (*sings*)   'Three little maids . . . ' (*Speaks.*) Yes, it's a Japanese-style garden.

Alan   Maybe we should . . . maybe . . . ?

Peter   Mmmm?

Alan   Maybe we should introduce some Japanese features into our garden.

Peter   I thought ours was a traditional English-style garden.

Alan   But a splash of Japanese −

Peter   Too complicated. Don't. You complicate . . .

Alan   Yes?

Peter   You don't need to complicate. It's English, there's no need to complicate.

Alan   Alright then. The new bench is alright?

Peter   Of course.

Alan   You don't think the new bench was too complicated?

Peter   I think the new bench is lovely.

Alan   I thought we were agreed, I thought we agreed that day at the garden centre that the bench was right, that the bench was lovely, the right –

Peter   We did. It is. The bench is lovely.

Alan   Well, I like it.

Peter   And so do I.

Alan   Just sitting on the bench smelling all those roses, it's . . .

Peter   Paradise.

Alan   Isn't it, yes?

Peter   It's paradise on the earth.

Alan   I'm glad we're . . .

Peter   So we don't need to add a splash of Japanese to that, do we?

Alan   No. No – you're right.

Peter   Of course I'm right.

Alan   You're always right.

Peter   I'm nearly always right.

Alan   You're nearly always right. (*Pause.*) Glad to have you around.

Peter   Thank you.

Alan   . . . Glad you didn't . . . pop off.

Peter   Ah well . . . not my time, was it? When my time comes . . .

Alan   Indeed.

Peter   When my time comes then I'll 'pop off'.

Alan   . . . I was the Lord High Executioner at school.

Peter   I didn't know that.

Alan   They brought in boys from the junior school for the little maids. I got a kiss out of one of them.

Peter   You never told me.

Alan   This was . . . it was so long ago.

Peter   To think there are still secret little maids after all these years.

Alan   Oh . . . There are millions.

Peter   Stud muffin.

Alan (*laughs*)   Good God. 'Stud muffin'. 'Stud muffin'. What about you? Have you got any secret little maids?

Peter   Secret little maids? Hah. I wish.

Alan   Any secrets at all?

Peter   Any secrets? Far too many secrets.

Alan   Well . . .

Peter   Well . . .

Alan   I spoke to the guy next door.

Peter   Martin?

Alan   With the SUV.

Peter   Martin with the SUV.

Alan   I spoke to Martin with the SUV and Martin told me that they'd just had a valuation. They've just been valued, they've been valued and they can get over seven hundred and fifty thousand pounds.

Peter   I see.

Alan   Well, what do you think?

Peter   What do I think?

Alan   Yes. What do you think?

Peter   I think it's an awful lot of money.

Alan   Isn't it? Isn't it? Isn't it an awful lot of money? To think that prices have just leapt . . . and Martin hasn't even done the work that we've done.

Peter   I didn't do any of the work. You did the work.

Alan   I suppose so.

Peter   I was in the hospital. You did the work.

Alan   I wanted you to have the ground floor en suite in case −

Peter   Ground floor en suite. And here I am walking around.

Alan   But actually the work will have benefited the property a fair bit. If we go for a valuiation.

Peter   Silver linings.

Alan   Silver linings.

Peter   Silver linings.

Alan   Martin's selling up. He's off to the countryside. Said he wants his children to climb trees and pick blackberries while they can. Makes sense, doesn't it?

Peter   I didn't even know he had children.

Alan   Oh yes, Martin has children. Two children.

Peter   You think we'd see the children.

Alan   Martin says the children are on computers while they're here but Martin's sure that in the countryside it'll all be tree climbing and blackberries.

Peter   Let's hope so. They could be the last generation I suppose for whom there's any tree climbing and blackberries.

Alan   What do you mean?

Peter   Global warming.

Alan   Global warming? That's a gloomy thought.

Peter   Sorry.

Alan   Oh well – we'll never know whether the globe warms. We'll be dead.

Peter   Much brighter thought. Much better.

Alan   Will it rain?

Peter   Not for a while. We're alright.

Alan   Such an unstable year. Rain sun snow rain. Random.

Peter   It's going to get more unstable. Floods, like the Bible.

Alan   We'll be alright.

Peter   I don't think gated communities are spared –

Alan   We're on higher ground. We're safe. Whole counties will go before we do.

Peter   That's alright.

Alan   Still be nice to . . .

Peter   Mmmm?

Alan   Sometimes I think . . . I don't know . . . the Dordogne.

Peter   The Dordogne? Do you?

Alan   Yes. The Dordogne. Be lovely down there. We could get – what? – eight hundred and fifty for the house, buy something terrific for a third of that in the Dordogne, lovely nest egg.

Peter   You've been planning. While I was in the hospital.

Alan   I wasn't used to sleeping by myself. I didn't sleep well.

Peter   You should have called.

Alan   The nurse said no calls after ten.

Peter   You should have ignored the nurse. I had sleeping pills.

Alan   I used to lie there and I thought, if he gets well . . .

Peter   I see.

Alan   Dordogne.

Peter   Dordogne. So that's your plan.

Alan   That's my plan.

Peter   But you've done so much work on the garden.

Alan   Yes . . .

Peter   Just when you've got the garden looking so lovely.

Alan   I'll miss it of course, but we'll have a bumper huge garden in the Dordogne. Ponds bridges lilies arbours follies gazebos orchards.

Peter   You'll be busy.

Alan   I'll get a man in. Little old Frenchman.

Peter   You've done so much to the house here –

Alan   Worth it as an investment. But really . . . what do you really think of our place . . . ?

Peter   I think it's fine. I'm fine as we are.

Alan   I did at the . . . We were both keen.

Peter   We were.

Alan   But now . . . a gated community is a little bit . . . antiseptic.

Peter   Which is good for you sometimes. If you're wounded.

Alan   I suppose.

Peter   If you've got a wound, antiseptic is the best thing.

Alan   Yes. Of course. But still.

Peter   I don't want to do all that moving over again after just one year.

Alan   I see, okay.

Peter   Moving's very tiring. Why can't you settle?

Alan   I really want to do it. The Dordogne.

Peter   No.

Alan   I really want us to sell up.

Peter   No.

Alan   I think the Dordogne might be a perfect –

Peter   No.

Alan   I'll sort out the move, you go and stay with Ian and Hilary for a month and I'll do all the –

Peter   No.

Alan   This isn't a whim. I have thought about this. You're healing. You're getting better. You're getting stronger, and in the Dordogne –

Peter   No.

Alan   – would just be the perfect place for –

Peter   Listen. You're wrong. I'm not healing. I'm not getting better. I'm not getting stronger.

Alan   Yes, and if you –

Peter   No, I – I need to be here – I need to be near the hospital – I need to – I'm not going anywhere . . . It's complicated.

Alan   . . . Yes?

Peter   Because it's come back. It's aggressively come back.

Alan   Aggressively . . . ? When . . . ?

Peter   They told me yesterday and –

Alan   Before the garden centre? Before we chose the bench?

Peter   Before the garden centre. Before we chose the bench.

Alan   They told you yesterday that it had aggressively come back and all the time you just went along with the garden bench and everything?

Peter   Yes.

Alan   Don't you think that was an incredibly selfish thing to do?

Peter   Was it?

Alan   Yes, an incredibly selfish thing to do.

Peter   I don't see how.

Alan   But – how could you not . . . ?

Peter   I wanted it to be lovely. I wanted today to be lovely. I wanted everything to be lovely. But actually . . . actually . . .

Alan   Are you frightened?

Peter   I should say I am frightened, yes. Are you frightened?

Alan   I am frightened, I suppose I am, yes, frightened. Do they say – ?

Peter   They never say, of course. They'll never tell you if it's months or whether it goes on and and on and on and on.

Alan   But you – do you want to live?

Peter   Oh yes. I want to live.

Alan   That's the most important thing, isn't it? That you want to live?

Peter   That's an incredibly important thing.

Alan   We'll have to treat it very aggressively.

Peter   Of course.

Alan   Fight back.

Peter   Absolutely. Yes. Fight back.

Alan   We'll fight it. Get right down inside you and take the little fucker on and send him packing. That's the way to do it. Isn't it? Isn't that the way to do it?

Peter   I suppose so, yes. Yes, it is.

Alan   Are you ready for the fight?

Peter I suppose so. I mean, I'm tired but . . .

Alan I love you very much.

Peter Do you know, I wish you had it. I wish you had this cancer too.

Alan Do you?

Peter If I'm honest I wish you had it too. I wish I could send it out of my fingers now and pass it on.

Alan You can't.

Peter No, this stays inside.

Alan But you want me to have cancer. What is that? Is that anger?

Peter I suppose it must be anger.

Alan Are you angry with me?

Peter I don't think I'm angry with you. No.

Alan What cause have I given you to be angry with me? I've loved you. I came to the hospital every day. I didn't sleep. I worked in the garden. I prepared the en-suite bathroom, all because I love you and I want you to live and our future will be . . .

Peter It's not you.

Alan I should hope not. I'm not perfect.

Peter It isn't only you.

Alan I know I'm not perfect but I am actually a very good person.

Peter On the train, hospital to home, before the garden centre, I was on that train and I looked around and those people – they all seemed so . . . hideous.

Alan People can be very ill-mannered on trains.

Peter They were laughing and talking. The children. The children especially were incredibly hideous.

Alan   No manners.

Peter   And they had their music playing and someone was
being kissed and someone was eating and I really wanted to . . .
explode.

Alan   Shout at them? Give them hell?

Peter   No. No. Not shout at them. Not give them hell. Not
like . . . I'm on the train. They're all so fat and stupid and
contented. So fat, so stupid, so contented that I literally wanted
to explode – like a bomb – explode. Explode like a bomb.
Wasn't that silly?

Alan   So you wanted . . . ?

Peter   I wanted to go BOOM. Go BOOM and carry them
all off, drag them down to Hell or something but just – BOOM
kill them all like that. BOOM.

Alan   I see. I see. Maybe that's a normal response.

Peter   A normal response? I don't know. Maybe it's a normal
response – possibly.

Alan   You've had such a blow. Learning that it's come back.

Peter   I suppose that must be it.

Alan   Learning that it's come back is such a terrible blow,
isn't it?

Peter   It is, isn't it? I would have done it. If I could. This . . .
thing . . . ticking away inside of me, if I could have detonated
it I would have detonated it, and I would have killed everybody
on the train carriage.

Alan   I think you should talk to somebody about that.

Peter   I'm talking to you about it.

Alan   Yes yes, you are. You're talking to me about it. But
maybe somebody else. Somebody who understands.

Peter   There'll be an explanation?

Alan   There's always an explanation.

Peter   Of course. There's always an explanation. I felt the same at the garden centre. I wished I could explode at the garden centre. I wished I could make everybody die at the garden centre.

Alan   You should have told me.

Peter   You were busy. You were choosing the bench.

Alan   We chose the bench together.

Peter   I suppose we did.

Alan   We did. We chose that bench together.

Peter   Of course – we chose that bench together.

Alan   And our home? Did you want to blow up our home? Our garden?

Peter   No. I was calmer then.

Alan   Well – that's something.

Peter   Do you know, I think it might rain. Shall we go back to the car?

Alan   Maybe we should.

Peter   I think maybe we should go back to the car.

Alan   What do you want now?

Peter   It doesn't matter.

Alan   I'd like to know. What do you want now? Are you ticking inside?

Peter   Oh yes.

Alan   I see.

Peter   I am. Just as much – maybe more than – yes I yes it's there tick tick tick.

Alan   And if you could . . . this beautiful garden . . . ?

Peter   This beautiful garden I would consume in flame. I would swallow it in one huge gulp and crunch – destroy.

Alan   The beauty here, the people here –

Peter   The beauty here, the people here would be gone. They would be nothing. All of it would be nothing.

Alan   And me? Our love? All these years –

Peter   – would be nothing too. Because, because this is so much bigger than that.

Alan   I never knew what a selfish person you are.

Peter   Am I?

Alan   You are an incredibly selfish person. And yet still you will expect, you will expect the visits to the hospitals, the sleepless nights, the – you will expect all of this?

Peter   I suppose I will, yes. I will.

Alan   Well, maybe I'll just go off, go off, find some little maid and off we'll go to the Dordogne and I will be selfish. Maybe that's what I'll do.

Peter   Maybe you will.

Alan   You will be so alone. Do you want that?

Peter   No. I don't want that. Do you think you could do that?

Alan   I could.

Peter   I don't think you could ever do that.

Alan   Maybe you're right.

Peter   We'll carry on. We'll sit on the new bench tonight if the rain holds off and we'll carry on.

Alan   Why should we do that?

Peter   Because that's what you do – let's get back to the car – you carry on.

Play Ten

War of the Worlds

*A **Chorus***: *the people of a city.*

— This is for you. We gather in this square for you. This is dedicated to you. You brave beautiful people. You unbowed children of freedom and democracy. This is our humble tribute to you. From our city to your city. With love.

Sound of a bomb blast.

— You have been bombed. We are sickened.

— We are yes, we are yes, we are really, really . . . sickened.

— When we – the news – we are overcome by – sickened.

— It's morning – I have my shower, I totally and utterly exfoliate, I juice and I put on the news for just a few moments and there it is.

— I know because the children are crying. We have just started to make love, which is unusual for us, when I hear the children crying. Not tantrum, not attention, not . . . a new type of crying like I have never heard before and I rush through into their bedroom, just stop making love straight away and rush through into their bedroom, and the children are there with the television on and you were being bombed. We are sickened.

— You are being bombed. Buildings are falling. The castle, a garden centre, a train, a theatre – they are each – a bomber just blew himself up and – the images are so sickening. And you are all dying and I feel how horrible that must be.

— I see a man on a stretcher. His face is . . . blood. The doctor cuts inside right there in the middle of the street. Cuts into him and manipulates his heart, manually – like – watch – squeeze release squeeze release – kept this man's heart going. And I, I, I . . . yes – I fall in love with him. I can't see his face,

the blood. I can't see his body – covered in some sort of
insulated . . . but still there and then I am thinking – I will show
you now – I was thinking (*demonstrates*): ' We are one, you and
I, we are as one and if, when you come through this, we will
meet and we will love each other and lead a very happy life . . . '
Of course you, he, that man dies a moment later. They pull
the blanket over his face and the doctor runs on to another
person who needs him. And I am overcome with grief. Isn't
that just the strangest . . . ? I am eaten up with sorrow for a
man on a TV channel who had thirty seconds on the screen
while I was eating my breakfast. Am I some sort of strange – ?

–   No no. We feel as you do. Here's the little girl – see? – the
little girl I pick out running away from the blast, running away
and she's a little black girl but she's been turned to white by
the ash from the blast. See? See? The little girl is running
towards the screen and I'm eating my breakfast and I call out
to her – let me show you how I call out to her – watch me.
(*Demonstrates.*) 'Come to Mummy come come come.' You see?
I am actually standing here in my kitchen and I am calling out
'Come to Mummy'. For a second I even feel like she could
push through the screen or I could reach through, only a
second, an insanity – what an effect those sickening images can
have on you.

–   I don't think I've ever seen anything so sickening on my
TV at breakfast.

–   We've never seen such sickening things on our televisions.

–   These are the most sickening things ever to be seen on
television.

–   How can you feel anything but totally and utterly sickened?
Do you feel sickened?

–   I do, I feel sickened and the children feel . . . I shouldn't let
the children watch, the children really shouldn't . . . but none
of us can move. Just . . . (*Pause.*) I cry as much as them and
then Thomas comes in and we all sit on the bunk bed together,
the whole family, and we all watch the kids' little tiny telly and
we watch the thousands and thousands of casualties and I see

a woman who looks like my mother, she looked so much like
my mother, my mother who the cancer carried off so long ago,
and this woman actually sends me a message through the
television, she sends me a message through the television and
she says – this is her message (*demonstrates*): 'I love you. I love
you with all my heart, I am so proud of you, my child.' Very
simple words, but words Mum never actually said – fair enough,
it was eating her up, that illness – Mum never said them, but
that illness was eating her up – but now that woman with her
body blown apart by the bomb is sending me a message through
the telly. So when she dies I cry actually, do you know more –
I never cried when Mum died so – Now I cry like . . . I cry like
this . . . Watch me crying for you . . . (*Demonstrates.*)

– You have been bombed. I cannot function, I cannot live,
I cannot work or eat or sleep.

– I go to work. I try to sell and buy and deal and do everything
I'm supposed to do – to analyse, to forecast, to initiate, but it's
not working because I am so heavy with this grief.

– This is me making love to my lover until I say: 'No please,'
and 'Please stop, please pull out of me. This feels so wrong. It
feels so wrong to be making love at a time like this – like there
is a dead person in the room. I cannot make love when there
is so much grief.' He pulls out of me. I'm so lucky because he
understands it, he feels it too. My lover feels the grief that
I feel. He is such a good lover. I call him three-shot Thomas
because . . . well, because. But now. Here we are. See us
watching you. Watching the footage over and over. So little
footage. Too few cameras for your pain. Over and over but not
enough.

– This is a little graveyard. The children have made this little
graveyard in the front room for all of you, for your dead
children, and now they spend the time there crying and holding
each other. My children cry for you like this – (*Demonstrates.*)
I do wonder sometimes, should I pushing them out – out into
the sunlight and say, 'Play, be children, for God's sake play,'
but I can't because we're all feeling, we're all feeling – Thomas
says – (Show them please.)

Thomas   I'm selling the company. I might . . . Really
thinking about it. Because what's the . . . what's the point of a
media production facility after this?

–   And I really can see what he means. (Thank you, Thomas.)

–   You have been bombed.

–   You have been bombed and nothing will ever be the same
again.

–   You have been bombed and what is the point of anything
in our lives? I want to drive to the sea, drive to the beach and
just . . . feel.

–   Here is your photo that I cut out of the newspaper. There
were so many photos of dead people. But you were the one
who spoke to me. I don't know why just some . . . Here is your
photo and here are the flowers I cut from the . . . Garden
flowers for you, and I bring them into the kitchen and then
I come in and now I cry and cry and cry and cry and cry until
I lie on the floor in the kitchen and now I will, I let out great
screams of grief. Watch me as I do this. Watch me as I do this
for you. Please see my grief. See it. Watch. Watch. See. (*Acts out
this grief.*)

–   This is the letter I've written to you. May I . . . ? My letter.
'I'm sorry you had to die. It is so wrong. It is so cruel. I saw
you at breakfast on my television. I'm sure other people love
you. I hope . . . ' (*Long pause.*) I'm sorry I'm . . . (*Long pause.*)
'I hope you have friends and family who love you and who are
grieving but I just want you to know that I, a stranger who is
not a stranger, loves you with all my heart and my life from
now on is dedicated to my grief for you.' I have written my
letter and I didn't know what to do with it and now I'm
putting it in this envelope just marked – see? – 'TO THE
DEAD' and – somebody take it from me please. Take it. Carry
this across the waters to the dead.

–   Everyone, please – come here – form a group, that's it, and
send a message to our sister city. Is that everyone? Yes? Can
we . . . look to the – that's it – and . . . together.

–   YOUR SUFFERING IS OUR SUFFERING. WE
NEVER FORGET.

–   And . . . press 'send'.

–   And now here we are. Here we all are. The city. Gathered
in the square.

A giant image played on a loop of the other city exploding.

A voice repeats over and over: 'Why are you bombing us?'

Black ribbons are distributed.

Some come forward and lay black flowers before the image.

Everything is videoed.

–   I'm so sorry. I don't know you. But will you hold me and
share my grief?

–   Of course I'll hold you. Of course I'll share your grief.

–   Thank you. This feels right, doesn't it? Isn't it right when
there's so much pain that we all come together like this and
hold each other and share each other's pain?

–   May I cry?

–   Of course of course – let it out – let go – drive it out of
you – drive the sadness out for all of us to see. Here – everyone,
see – look now – all of you look at this one woman – as I drive
the sadness out of her – come grief – come pain – come howl –
come – YES!

A huge cry of grief.

–   That's it. Again?

–   Later.

–   Anyone else?

–   For the moment I'm hollow. Please – I need to sit.

–   Oh yes oh yes oh yes this is the right thing to do. Can we all
join hands please? Everyone join hands? The whole city? Queer
banker trucker mum junkie immigrant second-generation

lonely celebrity wheelchair bohemian? Join hands – now.
Together.

– That's it. The right thing to do.

– Yes. The right thing to do. Oh yes. Look at our city. Look
at our city coming together now. All coming together. All of
you. No . . . there is no selfishness here. No 'I' right here. So
much time we waste on 'I' but here it's all 'we' and how noble
that makes us now.

– No more words. We go beyond words. Only music can
express our grief.

*Everyone's hands are now joined. Music is listened to. Maybe a montage
of images.*

– YOU HAVE BEEN BOMBED. WE ARE SICKENED.
WE ARE GRIEVING. WE FEEL PAIN. YOU ARE FAR
AWAY FROM US. BUT OUR HEART IS YOUR HEART.
YOUR PAIN IS OUR PAIN. YOUR WORLD HAS
CHANGED FOREVER. WE LOVE YOU. WE WILL
ALWAYS LOVE YOU BECAUSE WE ARE AS ONE WITH
YOU FOREVER.

– Goodnight. Sleep well. Our city has done the right thing
tonight. Sleep, the rest of those who have done the right thing.

– Tonight I think I will sleep for the first time since you were
bombed. I am so much – how can I . . . ? . . . Yes . . . lighter.
I'm lighter.

– Home now. Look at us. Over here. Back home. Shhh. The
children are asleep. I took down their graveyard in the living
room – see . . . all gone? They didn't object – and now Thomas
and I will finally make love on the carpet. This will be the
spot. Right . . . here, I think. And it will be the best we have
had for many years. He will come inside me. I'll allow it. I love
him.

– Now I will tidy up the flat. I'm going to take down your
picture. Can I do that? Yes. (*Does so.*) There. Should I have
done that? Yes. Now seems the time. It somehow – I don't
want to cling. I will always remember you but I won't cling.

–   Oh. I . . . Can't see my mother's face. Ever since she died I've seen her face, but now I . . . don't know, somehow she's not there any more. Please . . . let's . . . Show me the book of photos of my mother. (*A book of photos is produced.*) Thank you. Of course. Thank you. Here she is. Here she is on the bench in the garden with the fag in her hand. That's her face. Of course. But (*closes the book*) gone again. (*Closes eyes.*) No. Can't see her. It won't stay. Goodbye, Ma. (*Long pause.*) Bye.

–   Coffee. Good morning. Here is your coffee.

–   A new day. A new day and it's breakfast here, I have this – look – lovely strong coffee. I'm sitting in a really buzzy spot. Look at me. All of you – *regardez moi*. Attention. It's all buzz right here. I have a buzz job amongst the buzz people and on the way to my bzzz bzzz bzzz office I pop in for a buzzy coffee. Bzzzzzz. And there's the TV – over there – it's on – and you're on the TV and you say to me, this is what you say:

–   'Why did they bomb us? We are the good people. That's what I just can't understand, why would you bomb the – us – the good guys? We are good. We – hey – we shop. We bring up our families. We keep order in our society. Our elected representatives make wise decisions. We have core values: freedom and democracy. The world yearns for our core values. And as quickly as geopolitics allows we are bringing the world our core values – freedom and democracy.'

–   And I'm dropping my little gang at the crèche and the TV is playing amongst the struggling hordes of the teeny terrors and suddenly you are on the TV and you speak to me and you say to me, this is what you . . .

–   'My good brother was driving a good bus that morning. A good man doing a good job. But now he is dead. He died on the street in front of our good TV cameras. From my own kitchen, surrounded by my own good family, I watched my own good brother die. My grief runs very deep.'

–   On, I'm looking after my lover in hospital and the TV is on so loud. I move to turn off the TV but suddenly you say straight out to me:

— 'You wanna know who did this? You wanna know who did the bombs? I'll tell you. I'll tell you. The evil ones did this. They looked at us and they saw our goodness and it was a threat to their utter evil. And so they had to do this. They had to bomb us with their evil. Believe me, my friend, evil is strong but if the good ones come together we can fight the evil ones and we will win.'

— And I move away from my lover in his hospital bed and I move up so close to the television — like this I move — and you look at me from the television and you say:

— 'Evil or good? Right or wrong? The righteous or the wrong? The choice is yours. But the fight is beginning and you must choose. Choose, my friend, choose. God or the Devil. Here it is — good . . . or evil. The battle is beginning. Choose. Decide. With whom will you fight? Choose. Now.'

Pause.

— Choose.

— And I'm not quite sure why, but I — Oh, but I wanna —

— Really? So do I. I —

— Me too. Breakfast time and I —

— We, we we, we . . .

All laugh.

— Stop that.

— Stop. That is not . . .

Hysterical laughter.

Appropriate.

All the **Chorus** *are now laughing hysterically.*

— I'm sorry, I'm sorry, I'm sorry but you are so fucking, so . . . (*Laughs.*)

— You are so . . . stupid. (*Laughs.*)

– You are so . . . vulgar. (*Laughs.*)

– You are so . . . naive. (*Laughs.*)

– You are so old-fashioned. (*Laughs.*)

– You are so crude. (*Laughs.*)

– You are fat, ugly, thick, unsophisticated, idiot, idiot. (*Laughs.*)

– Freedom democracy good evil God Devil oh my God. (*Laughs.*) Oh my fucking God. (*Laughs.*) What kind of fucking stupid fucking children are you, you – (*Laughs.*)

– Ridiculous ridiculous ridiculous. Ridiculous.

– Good. Evil. You fucking stupid . . . Phantoms. I piss on you. Piss on you.

– FUCKING IDIOTS!

Silence.

– Sorry. Please. We're – so . . . Please go now.

Silence.

– Oh. How I hate myself. I really . . . totally . . . You were bombed only a few days ago. I am laughing at you. What a wrong person I am. What a monster. Why did I laugh? I'm so sorry. So bad. What I'll do now is . . . I will fold everything. Everything in the drawers, the cupboards. Fold them up really really neatly. The socks, the pillowcases, the . . . I'm folding till the laughter stops. Folding like so. (*Demonstrates.*) There . . . calm now, Why? Why did I laugh ? Well . . . quite frankly it's your own fault – you made me laugh at you – when you – you have – Why did you say such stupid . . . ? Please don't ever ever *ever* do the battle of good and evil shit ever ever again, okay? Okay?

– I want to – please – I want to feel that feeling I had before. That sad feeling. The one I had for you. So please – could you – thank you, run again the images of the bomb? Hello – are you listening? I want the images again. Thank you.

The images are rerun.

Isn't that sickening? They are sickening. That's it. Rerun and rerun and rerun and rerun and you see – look at me – I'm going to get that feeling back. Look at me getting that feeling back. It's coming. It's – are my eyes moist? Anyone? Can you see tears? (*Pause.*) It's got to come. Please. I want it to come. I want to cry like I cried before. Just to grieve for you. Where are the children? Someone call the children. Call to the children to come and watch the reruns so that we can all cry like we did before. Build the graveyard again. (*Calls.*) Kids! Kids! Thomas! Kids! Come here and . . . It's the images, kids.

Silence.

Thomas – where are the . . . ?

I remember now. The children and Thomas are playing swingball, there's a barbecue – they don't want to – and I watch and I . . . I'm . . . empty. Sorry . . . can't feel what I felt for you before. I really want to but I . . . Well, quite frankly it's your fault. When I see you on that TV spouting that, that yes, sorry – shit. You have stopped me feeling what I felt for you before. I feel – well – nothing. Nothing. Alright – turn off the images. Off now.

–   Ma on the bench in the garden with the fag in her hand. What a silly old woman she was. Puff puff puff fag fag fag. Cheap little bits of wisdom. 'Look after the pennies' . . . 'Do as you would be done by.' God, how I hate that stupid old bitch. The cancer came before I could tell her, but I hate her. How I wish I could have told her face to face: I hate you, Mother. You did nothing for me. Nothing but blight my life. Where are you, witch? Show yourself, Ma. Show yourself. So I can tell you. HATE. Come out. No? (*Pause.*) No.

–   Oh. These are terrible, terrible feelings. I want to . . . I say to my lover: 'Just hold me. Let's just be calm and hold each other and love each other,' because I have to feel that here in the middle of the world is some sort of sanity, just a . . . stillness, just a simple love and now – oh thank God – here is my lover . . . my lover. (*Embrace.*) Oh yes, yes, yes, yes, yes, we're okay. Everything's okay. Thank you. Shhhhhhhhhhh.

–   And I want to sleep but you're on my TV, and you're standing in a field of wheat, there's wheat as far as the eye can see and there's just a pickup truck and you and you're saying to me this:

–   'I am an angel. I shine in the pure light of the Lord's radiance. My wing has been torn in the bomb attacks. But I will fight back. It is always the duty of the good ones to fight the evil ones. There must be a war. Let the war begin.'

–   Yes, I suppose we will have to make war on the attackers. These terrible people who can just blow apart a civilisation will have to be attacked. Which I suppose is right. I suppose we'll have to do that. Oh well, I suppose we'll do that. We'll do it. Let's go to war. Okay. War – okay – yes – war war war agreed?

A reluctant, bored show of hands.

Okay. War.

–   On the TV now. The war's begun. Twenty-four/seven coverage. The kids watch it. I'm busy.

–   'You idiot, you fucking idiot. Angel. Broken wing. What kind of, what sort of shit is this? All the years I thought we had the same language but now you're speaking and you're speaking, you're speaking such, such, such, such . . . shit. Angel. Freedom. Democracy. You are – ignorant blind stupid bully and I hate you now – and I – Thank God you were bombed so that I could see how much, the truth will . . . how much I hate you.' (*Pause.*) . . . Oh. I'm scared of myself, that a person, a people, a person, that me, that I, that I could feel, that we all feel – Isn't that awful? Does anyone else feel: thank God you were bombed? (*Long pause.*) Anyone? Anyone at all?

One by one the **Chorus** *all come forward and show their assent with a 'Thank God you were bombed.'*

–   We all feel . . .

–   We all feel such terrible – to you who have been bombed we feel these terrible – sorry sorry sorry sorry – terrible feelings thoughts feelings, but really – honestly that is how we feel.

–   Kids? Kids. Sleepy time. Time to sleep. Sleep.

Sound of bombing.

–   You have been bombed. It's happened again. I see it again.

–   It's on the TV now. Listen. That's the children calling, 'Come on, Mummy, come come come.' They want me to see the bombing. I'll go to take a look in a moment. Just got to take these. Calcium magnesium iron. I've got the blend of fruits just right in this today.

–   You are being bombed. I am busy. I have a meeting with our viral marketing boys at ten. I hear the news but – excuse me – I have to move the car out of the garage.

–   I really want my stomach to feel tight. I really want it to feel like it has not the slightest bit of give in it. This an advanced mat work class. She really pushes you here. I really want to be pushed here. I really want my stomach to a level that it's never been pushed. This really is a great crunch.

Sound of another bomb.

–   You are being bombed again and again. It's everywhere. Everywhere you go. Everywhere on every media outlet we see that you are being bombed again. Again again again again. You are being bombed.

–   You are being bombed. I wake up. You are being bombed. I shower. I exfoliate. I prepare the fruit. You are being bombed. I juice. I turn on the television and you have been bombed again. The worst so far they tell me.

–   You run towards me. In your arms you hold your dead child. Your child is dead in your arms and most of her head has been blown away and you hold your child out to me like so as if to say, 'Oh help me oh help me help me.'

–   And I say – I don't say this in anger. I am calm. But please listen as I say :'You had this coming. Can't you see – you had this coming?

'You with your stupid bullying you had to . . .

'Somebody had to strike back somebody had to . . . '

–   You hold your dead child towards me and I say now: 'I am
. . . oh . . . pleased this has happened to you.'

–   I hate you and I am pleased that this has happened to you.

–   That is the most awful, that is the most terrible, that is . . .
no . . .

–   I am pleased.

–   Oh my God, oh my God. There is nothing now. We are
no longer human. We are . . . we look at this and we . . . please
. . . There is nothing of the human being of me now. Or you.
No humans left.

Enter **Man** *drenched in blood.*

Man   I am dead by rights. But if you just reach inside. (*Holds
up knife.*) Cut through my chest. Cut. Please. Find my heart.
Squeeze. Release. Squeeze. Release. Squeeze. Release. My
heart. If you reach into me I might live for just –

–   I can't.

Man   I'm a hero. You're a coward.

–   A hero. Yes you are. I'm an average, you're a – But now . . .
dead hero. I'm alive.

The **Man** *lies dead.*

–   I never turn on the news now. I never read the newspaper.
There's a war going on. But somehow . . . it's best if I don't
know about it. It does such terrible things. It disturbs my calm.
And I treasure that. My calm. Look at me being calm. I don't
want to hate you. I've worked on that and now I don't think
about you. It was a rather lovely day today I thought. And I
think . . . Yes. I think we could have a rather lovely day
tomorrow. Tomorrow. Lovely.

Play Eleven

Armageddon

Emma, Honor.

Emma   And He watches me.

Honor   And He watches me.

Emma   He watches me as I sit on the bed.

Honor   He watches as I count the numbers on the doors.

Emma   He watches as I look at the minutes on the clock.

Honor   He watches me as I check the buttons on my jacket.

Emma   He watches me as I pull my skirt below my knee.

Honor   He sees the sweat on the back of my neck.

Emma   He sees the redness in my face below the paint.

Honor   And I search inside myself: Should I go back?

Emma   Inside I'm asking: If I'm not here, if I run now to the parking lot and go home −

Honor   Finding a place inside myself where He's not watching.

Emma   There's no place inside yourself where He's not watching.

Honor   But there is no place inside yourself where He is not watching.

Emma   He sees that I am frightened but I can't go back.

Honor   He sees my fear but also . . . He watches as I reach out.

Emma   He watches as I take a taste of liquor from the tiny bottle in the tiny fridge.

Honor   He watches as I knock on the door.

Emma   He watches as I hear the knock on the door.

Honor   He knows the feelings I have for the woman behind the door.

Emma   He knows what I feel for the boy in the corridor.

Honor   And in time He will make my feelings known to me.

Emma   He knows but He doesn't tell me what I feel – that is still a mystery to me.

Honor   Love and hate, lust, disgust, violence, tenderness.

Emma   And in time He will reveal them to us.

Honor   In time I believe He will reveal them to us.

Emma   I must answer the door.

Honor   Why so long answering the door?

Emma   Give me your strength to answer the door.

Honor   Maybe He has led me to the wrong door.

Emma   He sees the trembling in my hands as I reach towards the door.

Honor   Hello? Hello?

Emma   Yes yes, I'm here.

Honor   Her voice is tight.

Emma   He wants to bully me with that voice. The door opens.

Honor   She is older than I remembered. Something to do with the light.

Emma   He looks like a boy there in the light. Maybe He is a boy.

Honor   And He knows that I am thinking of my mother who lived her life for alcohol and cigarettes and men who beat her.

Emma   And He knows that I feel old and He knows that I am suddenly ashamed that maybe there is the smell of liquor on my breath – the tiniest sip from the tiny bottle from the tiny fridge – but still . . . the smell of liquor on my breath.

Honor   And my mother died and she was never saved and I look at her and I ask: 'Can I save you?'

Emma   And I look at this boy and I think: Are you one of the chosen ones? Shall our shining faces see the glory on the day his light shines on the earth and he calls the chosen ones to join him?

Honor   And I say: 'Can I come in?'

Emma   And I say: 'Of course, yes.' And I think I see a camera turn and catch you come into the room.

Honor   From the ceiling in the corridor the camera turns and watches as I step into the room. He is in that camera as he is in all things.

Emma   I want to kiss you. I want to kiss you. I want to kiss you. He sees that and He sees how much I want to kiss you.

Honor   He has seen the dreams I have of you. Your body.

Emma   And He is watching my mouth, the lipstick bleeding into the lines around my lips, the tang of liquor still on my tongue.

Honor   In my dreams you were so much younger.

Emma   I am old and my mouth is ruined and I say, 'Excuse me.'

Honor   And I say, 'Sure.'

Emma   And I step into that tiny bathroom and I rip the cellophane from the tiny toothbrush and I squeeze the tiny toothpaste tube.

Honor   And I sit on the bed and I – hah – I sit on the remote control.

Emma   I jump. I jump at the noise.

Honor   A bomb blast. A bomb tearing through the fabric of that building.

Emma   The noise of the bomb is overwhelming.

Honor   And I call through to the bathroom, 'Sorry sorry.'
I call through: 'Sorry.'

Emma   But I can't hear and I call out, 'What? What? What?
What?'

Honor   And I find the volume and I turn down the volume
of the news of the bomb blast.

Emma   My gums are bleeding from the bristles.

Honor   And I say: 'There's been another blast. In the war.
The news is coming in. More of our boys are killed.'

Emma   And He hears my fear, as every day He hears my
fear, as every day my fear . . . as every day I watch the TV,
more bombs, more of our boys killed, more of our boys
fighting in his name.

Honor   And I flip the channels till I find a choir and they are
singing of your goodness and I sit and I watch them sing of
your goodness.

Emma   My mouth is blood and liquor and toothpaste.

Honor   I want to cry and shout and sing with the beauty
of your goodness like I always do. Oh praise you, praise you,
praise you.

Emma   My boy is in the war.

Honor   I watch you. He watches you. We watch you step
from the bathroom.

Emma   My boy is in the war.

Honor   Yeah?

Emma   'My boy is a fighter for freedom and truth and
democracy.' He is speaking through me now.

Honor   Well – hallelujah.

Emma   Hallelujah.

Honor   There's nothing finer than to fight for freedom and
truth and democracy.

Emma   It is his fight.

Honor   It is his fight.

Emma   Can I ask you . . . ? Can we pray? Can we pray that my boy is safe? Can we pray that my boy escaped this bomb and that he can continue the fight for freedom and truth and democracy?

Honor   And I say: 'I'd like that.'

Emma   And I say: 'Thank you. It's just a thing I do every time . . . '

Honor   It's what he'd expect.

Emma   It's what he'd expect.

Honor   And I take the Bible from the table beside the bed.

Emma   You look so beautiful lifting the Bible from the table beside the bed.

Honor   And He watches us as we kneel down and He hears us.

Emma   He hears us as we pray for my boy.

Both   O Lord, you have chosen our land to be the land of freedom and democracy. We thank you for that. O Lord, you have cursed our enemy with tyranny and poverty and our enemy has grown envious of our blessed good fortune. And our enemy has attacked our blessed country. And now we bring them freedom and democracy as we bring freedom and democracy throughout this world. Oh, ours is a heavy burden but we carry it with pride. For it is your will. We are the free ones. We are the chosen ones. We glory in thy light and long to join you in thy heavenly kingdom. Hallelujah. Hallelujah. Hallelujah.

Honor   You've been drinking liquor?

Emma   You see the bottle as He saw the bottle.

Honor   This is your liquor?

Emma   There was temptation . . . a little fridge. It was a test. I failed.

Honor   Oh, sister.

Emma   It was the smallest drop. I was frightened. I failed. Will you forgive me?

Honor   It's not for me to forgive.

Emma   I'll wash it away.

Honor   My mother was taken away by liquor. When things got slow at the canning factory, she took to drinking. By the time things were faster at the factory she was too deep in drink to ever work again.

Emma   I don't want to touch any more.

Honor   She would bring men back. She had sexual relations with them. They took many drugs. I was a boy. I was so frightened. I'm going to go now.

Emma   No no no. See. And I pour the liquor down the sink and I call out begone begone begone.

Honor   He saw my fear. And He called to me. He spoke to me as my mother never did.

Emma   He called me later. My body is sullied. It has known many men. I have spent years filling my life with alcohol and drugs and empty relationships. My boy left. We haven't spoken in three years. He said, 'You are no longer next of kin.' I was in the gutter but finally he called to me.

Honor   Does He want us here tonight?

Emma   I don't know. I have asked Him so many times.

Honor   But He doesn't answer.

Emma   He doesn't answer.

Honor   I watch you. At your booth. Taking the calls. Counting through the day.

Emma   I've watched you. Peered over my booth.

Honor   And at service, I see you arrive. I see your hunger for the word.

Emma   I see you. The ministry. There are so many families. And you seem so alone.

Honor   Thank you for agreeing to be here.

Emma   I don't know that I should.

Honor   I don't know. When there's no guidance . . .

Emma   I'm sorry that I'm so old.

Honor   You don't seem old to me.

Emma   You can be honest.

Honor   You seem old to me . . . but still I desire you.

Emma   Oh.

Honor   Yes, I have a great desire for you.

Emma   Surely that must be wrong?

Honor   I suppose it must.

Emma   It's my boy. O Lord. O Lord. It's my boy's face on the TV screen. And I kneel before the TV screen and I hear them tell me: 'Your boy has been killed. Your brave strong beautiful boy who was bringing freedom and democracy to a land where there was no freedom and democracy has been blown away. He gave no next of kin, saying he is all the father and mother that I need.' He is dead. He is dead. My boy is dead.

Honor   I'm so sorry.

Emma   That I should learn like this in this tiny motel room with a huge TV and liquor and blood and toothpaste in my mouth and a boy who I have batted and swayed at when we work at the call centre. This boy I have arranged to meet to do something we dare not name. This is not the way I want this to be.

Honor   I'll die in a just cause. For each of us there is a just cause at the right time.

Emma   There should be tears now. Bring me tears.

Honor   This makes me even more resolved in my cause.

Emma   I want liquor. I want drugs. I want gratification. If only they would fill me up now.

Honor   He is watching you. He is tending you.

Emma   I have been hollowed.

Honor   He forbids you alcohol or drugs or sexual gratification.

Emma   MY BOY IS DEAD! AGGGGGHHHHH! MY BOY IS DEAD!

Honor   Our nation is proud.

Emma   MY BOY!

Honor   A hero. He is with the King. He is at his right hand.

Emma   I WAS HIS MOTHER. I was his terrible terrible mother.

Honor   But more than that he was our nation's, he was our president's, he was our God's.

Emma   Tears. Tears. Tears.

Honor   And now there are tears and she falls to the floor this old woman and for hours she fills the room with her sobs and the TV fills the room and sells us beer and health insurance. And I pray a silent prayer.

Silence.

Emma   Thank you for your prayers.

Honor   Thank you for allowing me to be here. He spoke to me.

Emma   Yes?

Honor   He told me that it is right that I'm here.

Emma   Good.

Honor   This is a moment of huge trial for you.

Emma   And for the world. The good against the evil.

Honor   We'll win through. He is with us. Of course.

Emma   I'm going to lie on the bed. I'm very tired. I'm going to lie and . . .

Honor   Would you like me to read to you? I know a passage I'd like to share with you.

Emma   Yes. No. I'd like you to lie beside me.

Honor   And I lie beside you.

Emma   He sees the boy lying beside the old woman.

Honor   He sees the young man lying beside the old woman. And He knows what is in my heart.

Emma   And the boy's arm moves over the old woman.

Honor   Moves over the old woman.

Emma   And I am comforted. And the game show becomes a comedy show on the TV and the room is filled with laughter.

Honor   We are chosen to join Him in Heaven where we will live for all eternity.

Emma   We are chosen to join Him in Heaven where we will live for all eternity.

Honor   Why do you work at the call centre?

Emma   For the health insurance. I have diabetes. You?

Honor   Health care also. I have a history of depression.

Emma   I'm sorry to hear that.

Honor   So we're both little angels with broken wings?

Emma   How like my son he is.

Honor   And now I move my hand up her body and I slip my hand inside her shirt and I stroke her breast. Do you mind that I do that?

Emma   He sees that hand moving over my breast.

Honor   Do you mind that I do that?

Emma   I don't think it can be altogether the right thing to do.

Honor   I don't think . . . And my mind is filled with images of her body bending and twisting, laying herself open to me, swallowing me, offering . . . and I try to push those pictures so far down, down where He can't see. But He sees that. And I try to burn up her body, burn it away with flame, consume it until it no longer exists but always her body comes back to me.

Emma   How easy it would be to give myself to him now. How easy and how wrong.

Honor   Just to take both our bodies and push them together.

Emma   We are both such weak people.

Honor   If I had a bomb now I would blast us both apart rather than allow any sexual gratification to take place. It's what He'd want.

Emma   The vomit rises in me. The death. The liquor. His touch. I go to the toilet bowl.

Honor   Late-night TV. The images are so unseemly. I find a preacher and a choir.

Emma   My stomach emptied. I rub toothpaste over my teeth and gums.

Honor   Will you look at this ministry? This guy is good.

Emma   How much longer?

Honor   Eh?

Emma   How much longer before the final days when He fills this world with light and He takes up the good to be by His side?

Honor   In our lifetimes.

Emma   You're young. I'm old.

Honor   Very soon. Only a few more years. Do you hate this earth?

Emma   It's His creation. It's beautiful. But still . . .

Honor   It's not the shining glory.

Emma   It's not the shining glory. See my boy.

Honor   My mother was never saved.

Emma   I'm sorry.

Honor   She was a sinner. If you deny salvation . . .

Emma   Will you stay here tonight?

Honor   I can't. There's too much temptation here.

Emma   I understand.

Honor   Your body is full of . . . I wish it were more covered.

Emma   I wish everything in this world were taken away so that there was no temptation.

Honor   As long as we stay strong.

Emma   We'll get there. I want to be with Him so much.

Honor   Me too.

Emma   And the boy goes away and I stroke my breast just once before I lay down on bed and I sleep with the TV on so that a late-night movie becomes my dreams.

Honor   You have tested me.

Emma   You have tested me.

Honor   And I have denied temptation.

Emma   I was not tempted.

Honor   And every day we bring freedom and democracy to this world.

Emma   And the Kingdom of Heaven is oh so very close.

Play Twelve

The Mother

Haley, **Male Soldier**, **Female Soldier**.

Haley   You got up early. I don't normally get up this early. This is very early for me.

Female Soldier   Mrs Morrison –

Haley   Really – I'm a lazy cunt, I suppose. Yeah. Real fuckin' lazy. But you know.

Female Soldier   Mrs Morrison –

Haley   They call it clinical depression. But I don't know. Clinical depression? If that makes them feel better.

Male Soldier   Mrs Morrison –

Haley   Bone fucking idle, that's what I'd call it. Bone fucking idle.

Male Soldier   Mrs Morrison –

Haley   That's what I am. Bone fucking bone fucking idle.

Male Soldier   Mrs Morrison –

Haley   I'm a bone fucking bone idle bitch and I need some cunt come along give me a kick up the fucking arse and say, 'Get out the fucking place and look for a fucking job cos there's job's out there for those who can be fucking arsed to look.' That's what I need.

Female Soldier   Mrs Morrison –

Haley   I'm a cunt. There's hard workers and there's lazy cunts. And I'm a cunt.

Female Soldier   Mrs Morrison –

Haley   Does bad language bother you? I thought you being army . . . The army everything's cunt the other, right? I mean

when Darren come back he was all . . . Does it bother you?
Cunt cunt cunt cunt cunt cunt cunt cunt cunt.

Male Soldier   Mrs Morrison –

Haley   Cig? Go on. I won't tell.

Male Soldier   I give up.

Haley   Good boy. Your mum must be proud of you. Me too.

She lights herself a cigarette. Offers **Female Soldier**.

Haley   Yeah? It's better than a landmine, darling.

Female Soldier *takes cigarette.* **Haley** *lights it.*

Haley   That's it. Few minutes less on this planet, isn't it?
Gotta be a plus.

Male Soldier   Mrs Morrison –

Haley   Will you fuck off? We're enjoying a moment of
cancer here.

Male Soldier   Mrs Morrison –

Haley   Bet you got a tiny dick. You ever seen his dick? I bet
his dick's tiny.

Male Soldier   Mrs Morrison –

Haley   Bet you wouldn't even feel him slip in, would you?

Male Soldier   Mrs Morrison –

Haley   Oh, sorry, are you two together like – ? (*Mimes sex.*)
Sorry.

Male Soldier   Mrs Morrison –

Haley   Do you want breakfast? I might have some bread
rolls. I don't eat much. The pills they put me on, they, you
know . . .

Female Soldier   Mrs Morrison –

Haley   You could do with skipping a few breakfasts, you fat
bitch.

Female Soldier   Mrs Morrison –

Haley   You can kick me if you want. Insulting the army.
That must be worth a kicking. Come on. Who's first? What
is it? He gets me down but then you do the real damage, eh?
Is that it? Bet that's it? That's got to be it. Men got a bigger
punch but they fight with rules. But women – there's no
fucking rules, isn't that right? No fucking rules. I've not had
a scrap for a few years now but the girls, they were always the
biggest cunts. Come on. You kick me till I'm down and then
she can do the real damage. Tear a tit off. Come on, the pair
of you. I deserve it. That's what I deserve. Come on. No?
Fucking pussy.

Female Soldier   Mrs Morrison –

Haley   I'll get you a roll. Do you want anything in your roll?
Bacon? Sausage?

Female Soldier   Mrs Morrison –

Haley   Sausage, bacon, egg?

Female Soldier   Mrs Morrison –

Haley   What's it to be? What you gonna have in your
breakfast roll?

Male Soldier   Mrs Morrison –

Haley   I'll do a bit of everything and you can choose later.
You watch the breakfast telly while I – there, who wants to
push the buttons? – you find the breakfast telly, while I –

Male Soldier   No.

Haley   I'll only be a few minutes.

Male Soldier   No.

Haley   It's no bother. Really. I've got a microwave.

Male Soldier   No.

Haley   No? This is my house, this is my house, I worked
thirty years so don't you fucking tell me don't you fucking tell

me. You're not occupying my fucking house, alright, so don't
you fucking tell me –

Female Soldier   Mrs Morrison –

Haley   Out there you can march into any cunt's house and
torture the fuck out of the towelhead cunt but you're not there
now, you're here, and while you're here I got rights and this is
my house so don't you tell me.

Female Soldier   Mrs Morrison –

Haley   How old are you? How old?

Female Soldier   It doesn't . . . Twenty.

Haley   You?

Male Soldier   Thirty.

Haley (*indicates herself*)   Forty-three. Fucking old. They
shouldn't give you this job. Pair of kids

Male Soldier   Mrs Morrison –

Haley   You don't have to . . . job done. Go and buy yourself
a coffee on the high street. You don't need to . . . We can just
pretend you did it. I won't tell.

Male Soldier   Mrs Morrison –

Haley   What is it now? Starbucks? Go on – off you go.

Female Soldier   Mrs Morrison –

Haley   You spend half an hour in there, you watch the world
go by, you talk about what you saw on telly last night and you
go back and you say 'job done'.

Female Soldier   Mrs Morrison –

Haley   But do me a favour, yeah? Don't say I took it well.
I never took anything well. Say she took it fucking badly. No,
don't say that – say she, she . . . that's it! . . . processed it, say
she got it out of her system, she cried and we talked about all
the brilliant times she had with Darren. Say: she got out
photos from school and holidays, she took us up to his room –

which she was looking after lovely – and yes of course there
was lots of tears, of course there was, but still she listened and
she acknowledged. There was no denial. They hate that, if
you're in denial. So – no fucking denial. She didn't take it too
bad or too good otherwise they'll up the pills and they're
already making me feel like a mong and I don't want that. Say:
she took it about right. Can you do that?

Female Soldier   Mrs Morrison –

Haley (*to* **Male Soldier**)   I'm sure you can do that.

Female Soldier   Mrs Morrison –

Haley (*to* **Male Soldier**)   But I'm not so sure about her. She
looks a bit fucking thick to me. Am I right – a bit fucking
thick?

Male Soldier   Mrs Morrison –

Haley (*to* **Female Soldier**)   That what they call you, 'thick
bitch'? bet they do. Thick bitch. Thick bitch. Thick bitch.

Male Soldier   Mrs Morrison –

Haley   No, really, thank you. I'm alright. You've been . . .
I'll get myself a roll and egg and I'll watch the breakfast telly.

Male Soldier   Mrs Morrison –

Haley   Are you sitting on my telly thing?

Male Soldier   Mrs Morrison –

Haley   Which of you is sitting on my telly thing?

Male Soldier   Mrs Morrison –

Haley   Don't fucking mess me about. Come in here ruining
my day. I do breakfast roll and telly, then go up, get a bit of
dinner and my ticket – rollover week, so . . . then home for
dinner, a sleep, my quizzes. I like my day so don't you don't . . .

Female Soldier   Mrs Morrison –

Haley   Which of you's got my pointer? One of you's got my
pointer? Yeah? Yeah? Come on. Cos when I find out who it is

I'm gonna stick your fuckin' teeth so far down your fuckin'
throat. Come on, you cunts. Come on, you cunts. I'll have you.
I'll fucking have you. Who's first? Or together, yeah? I'll take
you both on together.

Female Soldier   Mrs Morrison –

Haley   Alright, you bitch, I warned you –

She goes to hit **Female Soldier** *but is restrained by* **Male Soldier**.

Male Soldier   Mrs Morrison –

Haley   You ain't gonna have tasted fist like this before, thick
bitch.

Male Soldier   Mrs Morrison –

Haley   Think you're hard but I'm hard as fuckin' – ow!

Male Soldier *has pulled her arm up behind her back.*

Haley   You're hurting.

Male Soldier   I'm restraining.

Haley   It's hurting, darling. Don't hurt me. Don't. Doctor
told me: take it easy. Take it easy, he told me, and he give me
the pills.

Female Soldier   Mrs Morrison –

Haley   He's strong, isn't he? I like a strong man. I've always
gone for a strong man. My husband was a strong man. Weak
heart but a strong man. You're hurting me.

Female Soldier   Mrs Morrison –

Haley   Tell him to stop hurting me. I got rights.

Female Soldier   Mrs Morrison –

Haley   I got rights. I know what you do. I know you lead
them around on chains and shit on them. But that's not here.
Here we don't do that.

Female Soldier   Mrs Morrison –

Haley   We're human beings here. Are you human beings?
No, I don't think you are. I don't think you fucking are.

Female Soldier   Mrs Morrison –

Haley   ANIMALS.

She breaks free and leaps around acting as a monkey.

Oo-oo-oo-oo-oo-oo-oo-oo.

Male Soldier   Mrs Morrison –

Haley *gets down on her hands and knees. She barks over and over.*

Male Soldier   Mrs Morrison –

Haley *howls at the moon.*

Male Soldier   Mrs Morrison –

Haley *bares her teeth and growls at him.*

Male Soldier *gets down and looks her in the face.*

Male Soldier   Mrs Morrison, it is my sad duty to inform
you that your son Darren Morrison was –

Haley   No!

She bites his nose. He leaps back.

Male Soldier   Fuck. You bitch, you fucking fucking bitch.

*He goes to kick **Haley**. **Female Soldier** pulls him back.*

Female Soldier   Hey no no NO!

Male Soldier   Fucking mad.

Haley *growls.*

Male Soldier   You're fucking mad.

Haley *growls.*

Male Soldier   See you? You're the worst I've ever seen.
'It was for his country. It was what he would've have wanted.
I wished his nan had lived to see the funeral.' That's what

you're supposed to . . . not . . . I wouldn't put you on pills.
I'd send you down the funny farm.

Female Soldier   Alright.

Haley *yaps.*

Male Soldier   Down the funny farm and chop inside yer
head till you could act normal. You wanna act normal you do.

Female Soldier   You're bleeding.

Male Soldier   Course I'm fucking – (*To* **Haley**.) If you're
infected I'll have you.

Female Soldier   Here.

She gives him a cloth to mop the blood.

Male Soldier   Ooooowww.

Female Soldier   Mrs Morrison, it's our sad duty to inform
you that your son Darron Morrison –

Haley   It's just the words, I don't want you to say the words.

Female Soldier   I have to.

Haley   Why?

Female Soldier   It's a requirement.

Haley   Big on rules.

Male Soldier (*still bleeding*)   Fuck.

Haley   Sorry, I just . . .

Male Soldier   . . .

Haley   No, I mean it, I do, sorry, not your fault, you got a
job to do. I know that. I used to have a job to do. Canning. It
was shit but you know . . . We all stunk of ham, we did. You'd
be after a shag but that ham'd be right in your skin and the
blokes'd be, 'You're a can tart.' Some of 'em didn't mind. Some
were picky. But still, you'd always manage to pull something if
you waited till chucking-out time, know what I mean. (*To* **Male
Soldier**.) Kiss it better?

Male Soldier   Fuck off.

Haley   Come on, I'm a mother, I know how to –

Male Soldier   Oh fuck.

Haley   Let me have a look. That's it, that's it. Oh you poor wounded boy you. What they been doing to you? (*To* **Female Soldier**.) Water.

Female Soldier   We really don't have –

Haley   Bowl of water, TCP, plaster. NOW.

Female Soldier *exits.*

Haley   Look what they done to you. Look what they done to my beautiful boy.

Male Soldier   Mrs Morrison –

Haley   Did they hurt your beautiful face?

Male Soldier   Mrs Morrison –

Haley   Shhh now shhh now shhh. They're jealous of you cos you're so lovely. That's what. Jealous and they hate you. They hate us. Cos we got good lives. We lead good lives. This is a good house, innit? You got a good room. I kept your posters up. Everything about our good way of life they hate so they bomb and they shoot and they –

Enter **Female Soldier** *with bowl of water, cloth, TCP, cotton-wool buds, plaster, towel – all on a tray.*

Haley   That's it. We're going to get you better. We are going to get you totally better. Yeah?

She washes his wound with the cloth and water.

All coming off. All going. Bit of a sting.

Applies TCP.

Brave boy.

Plaster on. **Female Soldier** *out with tray of stuff.*

Haley   No more fighting, eh? Yeah? Promise me? You did your bit and that was good but no more fighting now, eh? Just stay home for a bit. There's a new quiz on the telly. You'll like it. You stay home and watch that with me. Or go out and have a bit of a piss-up with your mates and then bring us back a curry, we can share that, yeah? Good old breakfast when you're feeling shit cos of all the drink. You'll love that. I'll love it. Welcome home.

Female Soldier *comes back in.*

Male Soldier   Mrs Morrison, it is my sad duty to inform you that your son Darren has been killed in action. Darren was a well-respected and well-liked member of his regiment who died as he lived fighting bravely for a noble cause. His CO sends you his most heartfelt condolences at this time of grief. Darren's belongings will be forwarded to you shortly. His coffin will bear the regimental flag if you so choose. Our country, our Queen, freedom and democracy will always be indebted to Darren for this sacrifice he has made.

Haley   . . . Were those the words?

Male Soldier   Yes.

Haley   Not so bad as I thought. You said them lovely. No, really. Really. Really. Really. Lovely.

Male Soldier   Thank you.

Haley   Well – you get practice. How many you do?

Female Soldier   There's further counselling.

Haley   In a day like? What's the record?

Female Soldier   In the home. At a centre. Or groups.

Haley   I'm not a joiner.

Female Soldier   A visitor?

Haley   I don't like people in the house. It throws the day. Who else you seeing today? Let him do the speech, he does it really . . . you do.

Female Soldier   You gonna be alright?

Haley   Course I am. You got kids?

Female Soldier   No.

Haley   Well. In time. You're young.

Female Soldier   I don't want 'em.

Haley   Want? Want don't come in to it. One day and your body's gonna need.

Female Soldier   Oh no.

Male Soldier   We gotta get on.

Haley   Every woman's a mother.

Female Soldier   No.

Haley   Mother. Blessing and a curse. Blessing and a curse. But you're gonna need –

Female Soldier   No, I ain't ever gonna, I'm never gonna. I seen too much to – never bringing a kid into this.

Male Soldier   Come on.

Haley   Course you will.

Female Soldier   No. The world ends with me. No kid. I'm breaking the cycle. It's too much.

Haley   Then what you fighting for?

Female Soldier   I suppose . . . nothing.

Haley   Have a kid, darling. Go on. Find a fella. Doesn't have to be around long. Have a kid. Inside you. Then out you: Mum, Mum.

Female Soldier   No.

Haley   I'll look after you. Babysit. Childminder. I'll support, I'll –

Female Soldier   No no nothing ever no fuck off witch witch –

Male Soldier   Hey hey –

Female Soldier   I ain't mother. Never gonna be mother. Don't wanna – just fight for my country and that's –

Haley   Mummy!

Female Soldier   FUCK OFF.

Male Soldier   Hey.

Haley   Right. Pointer. You put it down and then . . . I spend half my bloody time looking for that pointer. Really, I could go over to the fucking telly, but I get it fixed in me head, right, 'I had the pointer and now I got to find the pointer,' which is stupid, isn't it? But then that's me, isn't it? Fucking thick. You going out there again?

Female Soldier   Yeah.

Haley   Good luck. You're a smashing girl. What you got? Boyfriend? Girlfriend?

Female Soldier   If there's anything else we can do . . .

Haley   Ha!

She has found the television remote control.

It's always here. Sometimes right in front of your eyes – you gotta be patient. Right – fuck off the pair of you.

Female Soldier   We can make you breakfast.

Haley   Oh no. No thank you.

Female Soldier   It's not a problem.

Haley   I'm not a breakfast person. Cig'll do me.

Female Soldier   Maybe eating –

Haley   I – don't – want – to – eat.

Female Soldier   Right.

Haley *turns on breakfast television.*

Haley   This one is my favourite cos he's always on the lash
the night before, then he's doing his presenting but he fucks up.
I like it when they do the fuck-ups. That's my favourite bit.
One day he did so many fuck-ups they threatened him with
the sack. It was in the paper. But they knew he was popular so
they kept him on. He's alright, isn't he? I mean, I would if he
was asking. I definitely would. She's a bit of a cow though.
She's always in the magazines saying how much she loves her
husband but apparently she always fucking around. She loves
black cock, apparently. I mean, I can see the appeal but still.
She's two-faced. When they do bits on the war I flick to
something else cos I don't wanna know but they don't do the
war much cos it's all the same really, isn't it. Once one kid's
been blown up then what's there to say? It's all just body bags
and that's just boring really. They're doing ideas for doing up
rooms this week and I like the little poof does that. Think I'll
do up my room. Haven't done anything with that in years.
Purple's nice and a bit of a furry rug and there's mirrors with
beads round which is good. Oh – he's on 8.45 – that's good,
I haven't missed him. Oh yes – I like the little poof. He makes
me laugh. You gotta laugh.

The **Male** *and* **Female Soldier** *leave.* **Haley** *carries on watching
the TV. For a long time she is emotionless as the TV chatters on but
finally emotion comes.*

Play Thirteen

Twilight of the Gods

Susan *and* **Jane** *on either side of a desk.* **Jane** *has a breakfast roll and coffee.*

Susan   Do I get a breakfast?

Jane   You do.

Susan   I heard if I came here I'd get a breakfast.

Jane   You do, Susan, yes, you get a breakfast.

Susan   Do I get my breakfast now?

Jane   No, Susan, you get your breakfast at the end. There will be medical supervision while you eat your breakfast.

Susan   I'm very hungry.

Jane   Alright.

Susan   We've got no food in our zone.

Jane   I see.

Susan   There's nothing . . . We – we get no food, it's really –

Jane   I'm sorry.

Susan   So I think you should put that in your report.

Jane   If you like.

Susan   Yes I do yes I do yes – you write it down, you write it down and you put it in your report – my zone has no food.

Jane   Thank you, Susan, I will.

Susan   Do it now.

Jane   I'm sorry?

Susan   Let me see you do it now. Write it down. There is no food in my zone.

Jane   Alright alright, if that's what you want I'll . . . (*Writes.*)
Food supplies unsatisfactory in −

Susan   No no no, there is no food. There's nothing. There's
starvation. There's −

Jane   Susan feels there's no food in Zone Eight.

Susan   I know that. I don't − I know.

Jane   It's gone in.

Susan   You've got to let them know what's happening in −

Jane   I've noted the food situation, okay? The food situation
has been noted.

Susan   Malnutrition. Starvation. Gastro . . . We're being
taken away. Death in the −

Jane   Susan, I have noted, I have noted, I have noted the
food situation. Can we move on from the food situation?

Susan   If you like.

Jane   I do. How was the bus − ?

Susan   Can I have some of your roll?

Jane   My? Oh −

Susan   Sorry − just I haven't . . . It's been weeks since . . .

Jane   Of course. Yes. You −

Susan   I don't want to beg. I don't want to be a beggar like
this. I used to be an important person. I taught in the university.
I was respected by my students. I wasn't this pathetic − I'm not
this pathetic − But I'm just so −

She goes to grab the roll but **Jane** *moves it away.*

Jane   Susan − I'd rather you didn't actually, I'd rather you left
that roll alone. Now I've brought you here because I want you
to help me. I'm writing a report and I want your help.

Susan   I don't like being thin. I don't like having these bones
sticking out of me.

Jane   Susan.

Susan   But you – what do they bring into your side? Is it all special provisions for your side? Is that it?

Jane   No, it's just –

Susan   Look at you, you're fat, you're enormous, you huge great – and still and still you've got wobbling – and you sit there with breakfast you –

Jane   We are trying to get food to the zones.

Susan   To the victor the spoils, to the vanquished fucking fucking malnutrition, yes yes yes?

Jane   Susan, Susan – we want to bring you food, there is food, we are trying to bring food through – There is a world out there that cares and wants you to have food – it's important. Do you really believe the world is so bad?

Susan   No.

Jane   Good, no, the world is – only the insurgents stop us getting the food through, do you see? We try but we're attacked and we – It is not us. We are doing our best. But when there are destructive forces in your own people then –

Susan *grabs the roll and bites.*

Jane   Give me that. Give me that. Give me.

She grabs the remainder of the roll and returns it to the desk.

Susan *chokes.*

Jane   You see? You see? That's what happens. That's what happens. You see. If you just, just –

Susan *chokes.*

Jane   Here. Sip a bit of this.

Susan *grabs the coffee.*

Jane   Very, very carefully. Just a little sip otherwise it makes it worse. That's it, Susan. You're doing really well. You're doing well. I'm so proud of you. It's very important you – slowly, okay? You chew very very slowly.

Susan *chews slowly.*

Jane   We've had reports. People without food for too long, they suddenly get food and the food, the food, the food actually kills them, so could you just . . .

Susan   Okay.

Jane   We've got a report to write and we don't want you dying, do we? Eh? Eh? No, we don't.

Susan   No – we don't.

Jane   See . . . this report here. Man went off to the desert for six months. He got caught by the insurgents, freed himself. He made his way back to the city and found his wife living in a hole in the ground. She was a little shrunken creature. She hadn't eaten for months. And he was overwhelmed to see this woman – they'd both been civil servants – reduced to this . . . husk. So he went out and he bribed a soldier. Gave the soldier the last bit of money he had and he got this lovely red apple and he rushed back to his wife and he handed her the apple. And of course she fell upon it – it was food, but it killed her. Her body was so unused . . . It's all in here. Loved her. Gave her an apple. Hanged himself from a tree. See? All in the report. So you see – when I deny you things, when I say no, it's not because I'm some bitch who – I'm just trying to – do you see? We are learning, Susan. Mistakes have been made but we're learning from them.

Susan   Can I have some more coffee?

Jane   I'm not sure. I really don't know what the medical situation is with coffee.

Susan   We get water but actually all you taste is the sterilising tablets.

Jane   I'm sorry. I'll note that.

Susan   I really dream about coffee. I used to have coffee in the mornings. I'd leave the house early and drive across town to the university but I'd stop on the way for coffee and a breakfast roll. I miss that.

Jane   I'm not sure. Caffeine is such a powerful drug.

Susan   Tyranny was bad. I wrote articles. I protested. I did what I could. But every morning I had coffee and a breakfast roll.

Jane   Susan – I'd really rather you didn't have coffee without proper supervision.

Susan   If you think that's best.

Jane   I do, yes. I think that's best.

Susan   That's your privilege, isn't it?

Jane   I'm just trying to be kind.

Susan   That's your privilege. You occupy. You decide who gets the coffee and when they get it.

Jane   This really isn't some big political –

Susan   You say – pull the thin bitch in to help me write the report and the soldiers pull the thin bitch in.

Jane   I hope they were friendly. They did make clear this was voluntary?

Susan   Well – here I am and now you can do what you want with me because the power is all yours.

Jane   I really want to work with you.

Susan   I really want some more coffee.

Jane   I just want to do what's best.

Susan   Let me have some coffee.

Jane   That's why I came here – because I want the best for your country.

Susan   I won't drink the whole cup.

Jane   I saw how it was before on the television – the abuse of human rights and now the war, and I just wanted to be here to do the right thing.

Susan   Let me try a few sips – see if it's alright. It's not bread. It's not an apple.

Jane   Well . . .

Susan   We'll be very careful.

Jane   Well, alright.

Susan *takes a few sips of the coffee.*

Susan   Very good. Good coffee.

Jane   I think that's enough.

Susan   Very . . . Reminds me of civilisation, of having a civilisation, of normal things, of happy times.

Jane   Except it wasn't really . . . it wasn't such a civilisation . . .

Susan   No.

Jane   There was no democracy. No freedom. No human rights. There was massive infringement –

Susan   I know, but still . . .

Jane   You're in transition, Susan, you're a society in transition.

Susan   I miss the coffee.

Jane   Everything's going to get so much better.

Susan   Do you think so?

Jane   Twenty years' time you'll be leading the world – social and economic and freedom.

Susan   Can I have some more coffee?

Jane   I'd rather you didn't.

Susan   I see.

Jane   Just until we can be sure the caffeine – there's no ill effects?

Susan   No.

Jane   Well, that's good. Good. Well, if you'll help me with the report, you're going to get a supervised breakfast afterwards. A specially prepared purée, eaten under medical supervision. So that we don't risk killing you. We have learnt. We've progressed. How to move people on to food −

Susan   This isn't me, you know − this bony bitch grabbing at food.

Jane   I'm sure it isn't.

Susan   I was always big. I loved food. I loved to cook. I'd cook all weekend and then I'd have friends over from the university and we'd feast on a huge fish and lots of dishes and talk −

Jane   This was under the old regime?

Susan   You'd be careful what you talked about, but food − you could eat till your stomach swelled. I loved that.

Jane   It'll happen again. Once everything's settled down.

Susan   But now − one bite of bread and I'm choking.

Jane   I know I'm privileged, Susan, I know that I − I've been very lucky all my life.

Susan   I'm not judging you.

Jane   Alright.

Susan   You're being very good to me. I appreciate it. You're doing a good job.

Jane   Thank you.

Susan   I expect you miss your home.

Jane   Let's get on with the report.

Susan   Everyone would rather be in their own country, wouldn't they?

Jane   Sooner we do this, the sooner you get your breakfast.

Susan   Who have you got at home? Husband? Little boy?

Jane   I'm going to push on with the report. How was your bus journey?

Susan   I expect you're a very good mother.

Jane   Susan – let's move on with the report.

Susan   If you like.

Jane   How was your bus journey?

Susan   Why are we doing this?

Jane   Susan.

Susan   What is the point of the questions?

Jane   The point – the point –

Susan   Yes, yes.

Jane   Susan, I can still withhold your breakfast if I find you uncooperative.

Susan   I'm sorry, I'm sorry, I don't want to – no – I need to eat – but please, I'm an intelligent – I was once an intelligent woman. I have the kind of mind that asks questions. I don't want it to, sometimes I wish . . . I fought my father to go to the university. Sometimes I wish I was more . . . pliant. But I always – why? Why? Why? You see? I'm sorry. But if I can just understand what the report . . .

Jane   Alright alright. It's because . . . I suppose . . . I suppose it's because we've intervened, we've intervened in, we were impelled to intervene in, because of the terrible things that were happening in your country – human rights, et cetera – we felt impelled to intervene and now we – me – I and my colleagues – we want to find out how you think we're doing, okay? Since we've intervened, since the dictator's statue toppled, how do you feel things are going? We want to listen. Listen and get a picture. Alright?

Susan   You're a mother, aren't you?

Jane   I'm . . . look . . . I'm a foreign power. I'm bringing order. I'm bringing freedom and democracy, I . . .

Susan   My little boy's seven. He's called Dan. Before the invasion he used to play on a bicycle with stabilisers on the street with his friends. I've been living in the cellar with him for the last six months. Sometimes we enjoy ourselves. I make up stories. He makes up stories. The Little Devil. That's a character we made up. The Little Devil who – His friend with the broken wing –

Jane   How was your bus journey today? Any suspected bombs or bombers or other alarming incidents?

Susan   No.

Jane   Good, good. And how were the checkpoint guards?

Susan   How do you mean?

Jane   Were they helpful slash polite slash efficient?

Susan   One of them squeezed my bottom, which was –

Jane   I'm sorry. I'll note that. Sexual harassment.

Susan   He was a boy. I shouted at him. We understood each other.

Jane   It's important that we keep a record of sexual harassment cases. But otherwise – ?

Susan   Otherwise fine.

Jane   Did you find your bus journey satisfactory?

Susan   Yes.

She grabs the rest of the bread roll and starts gulping it down.

Jane   Susan, no Susan no Susan, stop that.

Susan (*mouth full*)   You have no idea, the hunger. The total, when you feel so hungry you –

Jane   Susan, stop that now. You must. That man. Apple. Hanging from a tree. Susan.

Susan (*mouth full*)   Food. Food. Food.

Jane   You fucking – I will not kill someone – I did not –
you grabbed that food – I came here – freedom – choice –
democracy – human rights – our core values.

Susan (*mouth full*)   Food. Food. Food.

Jane   This is not why I came here. A better world. You
grabbing grabbing – Oh Susan, what have you done.

Susan *begins to choke.*

Jane   Susan – I gave you every warning. I – I want to kick
you now, you know that? Kick your stupid – I brought you
freedom, you bitch –

Susan *collapses on the floor, choking and fighting for breath. This
continues during:*

Jane   I brought you your freedom. We fought our way
through the desert to bring you our core values and now
you can't even, you can't even – you grab like you've never
seen – oh fuck. What is the point? Shit. I look at the world.
Look at it. It's such a terrible place. So much terrible oppression.
Women in veils. Women with their clitoris cut off. Young men
brainwashed. People branded with hot irons for speaking the
truth. No elections. Rigged elections. I see all this. And what
am I supposed to do? Stand by? I've got everything. I've got so
much. I've got freedom, I've got democracy. I've got so many
human rights. Am I supposed to just stand by when the world
is in darkness? No. I have to intervene. I have to. So why does
it get messy? Why does it always get so fucking messy?

She takes a waste bin from behind the desk.

Susan, I'm now going to induce vomiting, do you understand?
I'll induce vomiting but please in here – okay? Let's keep this
orderly, alright? Alright.

Jane *pushes her fingers down* **Susan**'s *throat.* **Susan** *vomits into the
bin.*

Jane   That's it, Susan – all up, get it all up, you'll feel better
for that.

Eventually, **Susan** *slumps back and* **Jane** *feeds her coffee, cradling her.*

Jane   That's it, Susan, yes yes. Here we go. Susan – keep your eyes open. Just keep your eyes open – focus on me, Susan, try to focus on me. Try to look at me. Try to look at me. Open your eyes, Susan. Open your eyes. Susan, listen to my voice. Listen to my voice. Listen. Susan, I don't have a partner, a husband, I don't have a child. Susan, I have the most appalling taste in men. Susan, I pick men who hang around for a few months, I pick useless men with useless jobs, with pretend jobs, men who I support and then move on, they graze and then they move on. Susan, I think about having a child but that moment's going now, Susan, that's a little window that's closing – listen to my voice, listen to my voice – so the window's closing and I probably won't have a child, but I know people with children so . . . My flat is so lovely, Susan, I'm really making my flat the most lovely place. I love magazines with really beautiful interiors in them and that's what my flat is like, like a magazine interior and one day I think it will be in a magazine interior. I really think that one day. One day you'll get a new university so beautiful all chrome and glass and so much inward investment and you and your students will be able to speak freely just like our students speak freely. Susan, that's really going to be fabulous. I'm very optimistic, Susan, because everything is working out – the plans are in place, the infrastructure, the investment, the – freedom and democracy, freedom and democracy.

Susan's *eyes close.*

Jane   Open your eyes, Susan, open your eyes. Susan, Susan – open your eyes.

Play Fourteen

Paradise Lost

Liz, Ruth.

Liz I couldn't sleep. It's been several nights now and I . . .
my sleep is rather special to me . . . I think it is, isn't it? . . .
I think sleep is really rather special . . . such a healing thing . . .
I totally believe in eight hours . . . I'm a great believer in . . .
and so I've really been rather disturbed . . . you see . . . I
thought for several nights it was a fox, an urban fox . . . then
I thought, yes, an urban fox in some sort of pain, always at the
same time, the same pain the same time seems . . . I thought:
really I ought to be out in the garden looking for the fox but
really . . . really I wouldn't know what to do for a fox, so I tried
to block out the fox . . . I have earplugs, sleeping pills and a
CD of the waves which often . . . But then after a week or so
I thought maybe it's cats. I've never had cats so . . . I mean
I don't know much about the sound of cats but . . . I think
the female cat does make a terrible . . . Isn't it strange how in
the natural world the female of the species makes a sound of
great pain when she is being made love to? . . . I've always
thought that was very strange . . . you would have thought . . .
So I thought leave it, leave it, leave it, leave it, leave it . . . it's
a lady cat and she's having the time of her life. Lives. (*Laughs.*)
Lives . . . but I suppose actually, you know . . . I have a great
problem being honest with myself. I never tell myself the
truth . . . which is why I suppose nothing's ever worked
out on the relationship . . . I have terrible troubles with self-
deception . . . but a couple of nights ago . . . the scream, the
scream comes, and I said to myself if you're honest . . . if
you're honest with yourself . . . just be honest with yourself . . .
you know where that scream's coming from, you've always
known where that scream's coming from. That scream is
coming from the flat downstairs. That terrible scream in the
middle of the night is coming from the flat downstairs. Is it
you screaming? Is it?

Ruth   . . .

Liz   I haven't been down before because I didn't want to invade
your privacy . . . privacy is so important, I know . . . and . . .
but you are keeping me awake . . . I'm Liz by the way . . .
I know we've never actually . . . You always look very busy so
I never want to . . . anyway, I'm Liz. I'm Liz. I'm Liz. And
I know you're Ruth because I've seen it on the letters in the
hallway. Sorry. I'm not a snoop. But you can't help noticing.
You notice the names when you're looking for your post, so
I know you're Ruth. Is it you, Ruth, screaming in the night?
Is it? Because I've never noticed any other . . . and it's certainly
a female scream and it's certainly happening down here so
I think . . . I think . . . I think it is you, Ruth, screaming out
in the night. If it's not, tell me now and I'll . . . Listen, Ruth,
I don't want to invade your privacy any longer, I've invaded
your privacy for long enough so I'll . . .

She makes to go, comes back.

I work for an airline, Ruth. I work very unusual shifts. I whizz
all over the globe at very strange times of the day. So my sleep
is terribly important. It's terribly important. The airline are
very strict about – us girls have to look a certain way and if
I've been up all night because you've been screaming then . . .
do you see? Do you see? Could you just give it a rest because
my sleep patterns are disturbed enough without . . . ? Is it a
fella? I'm not a prude . . . I do know what goes on . . . I mean,
if you're into that side of things then fine, fine . . . You hit
him, let him hit you . . . we're all consenting adults . . . Who
knows, maybe I'd go there with the right fella . . . but at two in
the morning . . . two in the morning when I have to be in the
airport at six . . . great screams at two in the morning . . . that's
not on . . . This is such a terrible conversion . . . they charge
you, you pay over the odds, such a terrible conversion . . . I'm
sure you can hear me take a piss in the night. I know you hear
me take a piss in the night. I try to make my way around the
flat as quietly as possible after eleven . . . eleven o'clock is my
rule, so I'd be grateful if you . . . Yes, Ruth, yes? Yes? Yes? Just
you and whatever fellas or whatever you have in here, just as

long as . . . Can you tell them that? You tell them that, Ruth, yeah? Please, Ruth, please.

Ruth *sobs.*

Liz   Does he beat you, Ruth? Is he abusive? Is that what it is? Are you in an abusive relationship? So many women are in abusive relationships. I've been lucky I've never . . . but so many men . . . so many men . . . they think they love women but actually, actually they hate women, don't they? I think to a certain extent almost all men hate women. I really do. Well, what you have to do, Ruth, is tell him: no more, out, the door is barred. And if he won't listen then maybe you'll have to go into a refuge for a while, maybe that would be best . . . maybe if you looked online . . . there are places of refuge for battered women . . . Don't cry, Ruth, don't cry, there are plenty of places of refuge for battered women. Is he here now, Ruth? Is he here now? Is he?

Ruth *sobs, shakes head.*

Liz   Then you stop all the tears, you get into bed, you stop crying and you get some sleep. In the morning you change the locks and if there's any more bother from him — into a shelter for battered women you go, you see? Yes. Now — goodnight, goodni— good morning. I have an incredibly early flight so good morning and let's both try to get some sl—

Ruth (*grabs* **Liz**)   No.

Liz   Don't do that, Ruth, that's a silly thing to do. No, Ruth, no, I don't want you to do that. I don't like you doing that. Will you stop doing that, Ruth? That's not a nice thing to do. Let go of me, Ruth. Let go of me. Let go OF ME!

A struggle before she gets **Ruth** *off.* **Ruth** *sobs.*

Liz   I'm sorry, Ruth, but I don't want to get involved in your life. I just can't get involved. It's too much for me to get involved in. I won't get involved. No. I have such a busy life. Many, many, many countries I can't possibly . . . I just can't . . . you have to take responsibility for yourself, Ruth . . . you have to take responsibility for your own life . . . Sooner or later we all take responsibility for our own lives . . . that's it, isn't it? You share a lovely building like this and you try to be pleasant, you try not to disturb, you smile if you pass on the . . . But at the end of the day you take responsibility for your own life.

Ruth *seems calmer.*

Liz   There we are. Good girl. That's better now. That's much better now. I'm going now. I'm going to my bed. And I . . . Please, I don't ever want any more screams in the night, I don't ever want to be woken in the night, I don't ever want to come down here again – You've got a lovely place but I don't ever want to come down here again. Goodnight.

Ruth *pulls up her sleeve.*

Liz   What's that, Ruth? What's that?

Ruth *comes closer.*

Liz   Is that a burn? Have you burnt yourself? That's a nasty burn you've got there. Did he do that? I think you should go into a refuge if he did that. Are you harming yourself, Ruth, is that it? Do you hate yourself, Ruth? Is there a lot of self-hatred? Are you applying a hot iron to your arm and screaming in pain? I wish you wouldn't do that . . . I wish . . . This is . . . you smell of . . . this place smells . . . I wondered . . . But actually this place stinks of burning flesh. Oh dear, Ruth. Oh dear . . . oh. You bathe that, yes, you make sure you bathe that before you go to bed. Bathe it and bandage. Bathe and a bandage and try to get to sleep. Then you go to the hospital in the morning. They'll sort you out. Everything will get sorted out at the hospital.

She turns to go. **Ruth** *tugs at her.*

Liz   Ruth, no, please please please, I know something awful is going on here . . . I know that . . . I know . . . but I honestly, I honestly, I honestly . . . oh please, Ruth, I honestly can't get involved.

Ruth *falls to her knees.*

Liz   No, don't do that. That's terribly undignified. That's silly.
That's just silly. That's not doing anybody any good. You're not
doing anybody any good by . . . Come on, Ruth, come on . . .
Oh . . . listen, another time, maybe we can talk, maybe we
can . . . but tonight, this morning . . . I'm just so tired, just this
morning I'm just so tired and I . . .

Enter **Gary** *and* **Brian**.

Liz   What are you doing here?

Gary   Taking care of Ruth.

Brian   That's right. We're taking care of Ruth.

Liz   Who are you?

Gary   It doesn't matter.

Liz   I'd like to know.

Brian   He's right. It really doesn't matter. It really doesn't
matter.

Gary   How's she doing? How are you doing, Ruth?

Liz   I'd like to know who you are.

Brian   Just doing our job. That's all we're . . . doing our job.

Gary   Come on, Ruth, up you come, you remember me, you
remember me, don't you? Hello, Ruth. You remember me.
And you remember my partner.

Liz   What is your job? I'm sorry. I'd like to know what your
job is.

Gary   Well, here we are, Ruth, we're back. Both of us back.

Brian   We're both back to see you.

Gary   Did you expect to see that? Did you? Did you expect
to see both of us back so soon?

Liz   I still don't understand . . .

Gary   It's alright, we can handle the situation. We'll handle
the situation from now on. Where should you be now?

Liz   Well . . .

Brian   Where would you like to be?

Liz   Upstairs in my bed. In my bed in my flat. In my bed in my flat with a CD of the waves playing.

Gary   Then that's what you do, that's what you do, Liz. You go back to your flat upstairs and listen to a CD of the waves playing.

Liz   You know my name.

Brian   There's been post in the hallway, Liz. We haven't been snooping, but when there's been post in the hallway . . .

Liz   Of course . . . of course . . . I see . . . I see.

Gary   How are you doing there, Ruth? How's your memory? How's your memory tonight? Your memory any better tonight?

Brian   Go on then, Liz. Go on. Bed. Waves. Go on. No need to get involved here – nothing for you to get involved in here.

Liz   Of course.

Gary   I think your memory is gonna be much better tonight, Ruth.

Brian   You look tired, Liz.

Liz   Do I?

Brian   A bit . . . haggard. You get those waves on before you get too haggard.

Liz   Alright.

Brian   Goodnight, Liz.

Gary   Night.

Liz   Goodnight.

She starts to go.

Gary   Hello there, Ruth. What are you going to tell us? What would you like to tell us tonight? Are you going to tell us anything tonight? Come on, Ruth.

Brian   Come on.

Ruth *screams.* **Brian** *covers her mouth.*

Gary   Ruth, shhh shhh shhh.

Liz   Do you know anything about the burns?

Gary   I'm sorry?

Liz   There's a burn . . . a . . . branding . . . on the arm . . .
just above the . . . see?

Gary   No.

Liz   Sorry?

Gary   I don't see that.

Liz   Yes, look it's here, it's here . . . here there's a . . . you see?

Gary   I'm sorry, no . . .

Liz   But you must see −

Gary   Liz, Liz, Liz . . . I learnt . . . I learnt . . . I learnt a long
time ago . . . we are all disgusting, we're disgusting people . . .
We're not even people, we're −

Liz   I think she's in pain.

Gary   We are each of us so horrible, so horrible . . . there's
nothing . . . no animal, no devil . . . not the Devil himself . . .
We are all so horrible.

Liz   I thought maybe you could take her to the hospital or
something or something she −

Brian   She wants us to get involved. Won't get involved. But
wants us to −

Gary   Listen, listen, listen, LISTEN, I'm speaking, I'm
speaking. We're all so disgusting. There is nothing about us
that is not . . . Hell. I'm disgusting. I disgust myself. The things
I do are . . . the things I do are so disgusting. But we have to . . .
I have a wife, I have children, there's a mortgage, we . . . you
know, visit the garden centre, eat linguine . . . I'm a normal
guy, you know, at the end of the day I pay my mortgage and

I'm a normal guy so . . . I have to carry on. I have thought –
hang yourself. Of course . . . at times . . . hang yourself from a
tree . . . but when you go down and there's a perfectly ordinary
wife and perfectly ordinary kids and you're . . . oooh . . .
drinking coffee then . . . you have to carry on. Because that's
what you do. That's what you do. You carry on. And if you're
going to carry on you can't, you can't let it, can't let it . . . So
this arm, this arm . . . No. I look at this arm and . . . no.

Liz   But surely you – she's –

Gary   No.

Liz   Somebody has branded her.

Gary   No no no no no no no no. There's nothing there. You
don't see anything. There's nothing to see. Otherwise how are
you going to . . . ? You have to live with yourself and that's
hard enough to do without seeing . . .

Brian   Come on now, Liz, it's getting   Liz, come on, time
you were in bed.

Liz   Ruth – would you like me to stay? If you'd . . . if you
really want me to I'll stay.

Brian   I don't think that will be –

Ruth (*nods*)   Mmmm.

Liz   She wants me to stay. So if you don't mind, if you don't
mind, I'm going to stay . . .

Gary   There'll be nothing to see, Liz. There's never anything
to see.

Liz   I'm sure, but still . . .

Brian   We're just doing our job.

Gary   We're not bad men. We're not evil. We're no worse
than . . . There's lots and lots of, so many men like us . . . Yes,
we're disgusting, yes, the – Yes, I wish – The world isn't
perfect, I wish the world was perfect. I'm disgusting. I feel
guilty. I hate myself.

Brian We have to do our job.

Ruth *screams.*

Brian No, don't, Ruth, no don't, no –

He slaps her hard about the face.

Liz No. No. No. I – please – I don't want you to do that.

Brian That's a horrible noise, Ruth. Ruth – what a terrible noise.

Ruth *screams.* **Brian** *punches her in the nose.*

Liz No, that's – now that is – just you – stop now – stop, stop. She's bleeding, she's bleeding, she's bleeding. Come on, Ruth. It's alright. I'm here, I'm here. Liz from upstairs. Liz. Look at me, Ruth. You must have seen my post in the hallway. Liz from upstairs who works for the airline. Come on, Ruth.

Gary Look, I know this is upsetting, Liz. It's upsetting for all of us. So if you'd rather go upstairs –

Liz No.

Brian I think you better go upstairs, Liz. Go on, Liz.

Liz No, I'm – Ruth wants me – no!

Brian Alright.

He starts to unpack a tool bag.

Liz What's all that?

Brian Tools of the job.

Liz I see.

Gary Just recognised . . . Not under ordinary circumstances . . . but under extraordinary circumstances . . . Under extraordinary circumstances . . . The tools of the job. If we lived in ordinary times then, lovely – lovely times – all Monteverdi and linguine – lovely – but we don't, we live in extraordinary –

Liz The bombs.

Gary   Exactly, thank you thank you thank you, the bombs. They're bombing us. They hate us and they're bombing us and our freedom and our democracy so, so . . .

Brian   Extraordinary measures.

Gary   Extraordinary measures.

Brian *takes a hammer and breaks one of* **Ruth**'s *knees. She screams.*

Liz   No, don't, she's a person, she's a person, she's . . . No, don't do that . . . you musn't do that.

Gary   Have you lost anybody in the bombs, Liz?

Liz   Please, she –

Gary   Who have you lost?

Liz   The attack on the hospital. My friend was . . . Her boyfriend was in the hospital . . . sleeping by the bed . . . most nights by the bed . . . most nights . . . because she loved that man so, too, so much . . . and then the guy, the bomber, the kid, bomber kid, walks in one day, walks in one day, walks in and out they go, out they go, out they . . . The kid burns them all to Hell.

Gary   We've all lost somebody. We're all hurting. Does Brian seem brutal to you?

Liz   He . . . yes . . . very brutal.

Brian   I know I am. I hate that. I'm sorry.

Gary   He is. Brutal. I'm brutal. You're brutal.

Liz   No.

Gary   Liz, you're just as . . . We're all brutal and we're all hurting inside. Brutal and hurting, that's us.

Brian *swings the hammer at* **Ruth**'s *other knee. Screams.*

Liz   Stop it please stop it please no that's enough now you've gone far enough now stop stop stop.

Gary   Liz, do you know Ruth, do you know anything about Ruth, do you know who she is?

Liz   I've . . . I've seen her post . . . I've smiled . . . we've never spoken but . . . I've . . . She's been here a year so you . . .

Gary   Ruth hates you, Liz. Ruth hates everything about you. Everything about your way of life. Ruth would like to bomb you. Ruth is planning to bomb you. She's planning and she . . . She's been training and scheming and consulting and . . . She knew the hospital guy, she knew the guy who took out your friend . . . She knew him and now she'd like to take out you. She doesn't believe in justice and freedom and democracy, she . . .

Liz   No, I don't believe. It's not tr— Look at her . . . normal.

Gary   Ask her. She'll tell you.

Liz   She's like me, a normal –

Gary   Ask her.

Liz   Is this true? Is this true what he's saying?

Ruth   . . . Yes.

Liz   No, Ruth, don't.

Ruth   All true. And I say: fuck you. And I say: fuck your world.

Liz   Please. No.

Ruth   And fuck your friend who died in the hospital, fuck the people of this fucking –

Liz   Shut up. Shut up. (*She covers* **Ruth**'*s mouth.*) Shut your – Bitch.

Brian   She's got the names. We need names.

Liz   Give him the names, Ruth. Cooperate. Civilisation.

Ruth *shakes her head.*

Brian *gives* **Liz** *the hammer.*

Brian   Go on, Liz, have a bash. Have a bash.

Liz   Yes, I will. Thank you. For my friend.

Brian   And freedom and democracy.

Liz   For my friend and freedom and democracy, yes, civilisation, you will give us the names, you –

She goes to swing the hammer. **Ruth** *screams.* **Liz** *stops.*

Liz   I . . . no. Thank you. But no. I don't want to get involved thank you.

She hands the hammer back.

I really don't want to get involved.

Brian   You go to bed, Liz. Put the waves on and get into bed.

Liz   I will – thank you.

Brian   And we'll try to keep the noise down.

Liz   Would you? I'd be really grateful. Thank you.

Brian   Not long now. Not long now and she'll snap.

Liz   Alright. Alright. Alright. Goodnight.

Brian   Alright, Liz. Goodnight, goodnight.

Gary   Goodnight.

Liz *goes.*

Gary   Now then, Ruth – where were we?

Play Fifteen

The Odyssey

A chorus of **Soldiers**.

— We are leaving you now.

— Our planes are waiting, the convoy is prepared and we are going.

— Goodbye.

— I don't think . . . I'm sorry but I don't think you've ever engaged with us as people. But we are. People. I know I am. I'm a person.

— We are each and every one of us a person.

— Maybe you don't have such a sense of that, maybe your society is more . . . maybe your society is different in some fundamental . . .

— My little boy has grown up. He has a girlfriend. He messaged me. My little boy with a girlfriend. It's quite incredible.

— My wife tells me she's been faithful all this time. Every night she messages me: 'I love you, I pray for you, I am faithful to you.' She tells me that so I suppose it must be true but . . . she works in a call centre. There's lots of kids. Young kids. Young boys who are there for a few months making a little money taking the calls. The sight of an older woman. The challenge. I hope they've been kind to her. I love her very much. We love each other very much. But temptation. She's very weak.

— There's a garden bench I want to sit on. Very simple. Sit on the bench in the garden. So simple. But when there's been shelling and bombing . . .

— Maybe you can't imagine this, but there is no shelling and bombing in our cities. Our cities are beautiful places. Beautiful shops. Leisure facilities. People who move about in freedom, every day making the democratic choices that shape their future.

—   Doesn't that seem incredible? I can hardly believe it myself. It's been so long, I can hardly believe it myself.

—   But it's true. It's true. It's true. I remember the . . . oh, the power and the thrill and the beauty of the . . . choice. We have so much choice. Who will provide my electricity? Who will deliver my groceries? Which cinema shall I go to? There is a choice at home. I long to be back.

—   You haven't known that yet but you will one day.

—   What will be ours in twenty-four hours will be yours in . . . there's no easy path . . . but Hope and Belief and Love will take you there as they surely must take everyone there.

—   You will get there. Everyone gets there.

—   Oh, the path is long but please believe, believe, believe

—   Our pilots are testing their engines. They are in radio contact with air control. We will be leaving very soon.

—   The welcome that we will have back home. My wife will welcome me and we will make love as we haven't done since the first few happy months of our marriage.

—   My boy will call to me: 'Come and play on the Xbox, come and play on the Xbox!' And we'll sit together and play for days on end.

—   We will be heroes. We will be thanked and saluted. We will be rewarded. So few are prepared to dedicate themselves to the battle for freedom and democracy —

—   Freedom and democracy —

—   Freedom and democracy —

—   — as we have dedicated ourselves to the battle for freedom and democracy.

—   But our core values are everything because they are humanity's core values.

–   Do you see that now? Do you see it? Oh, please don't tell us our time has been wasted.

–   Surely our time hasn't been wasted? Only when I look at you . . .

–   When I look at you, you seem so beaten and so . . . You seem like a little husk. Like there's no person there at all.

–   Sometimes you look at me with dead eyes and I think I read, I, I, I . . . maybe . . . project, I project hate in your eyes. I used to see an analyst when I was . . . back home. I would drive across the city very early before the day had begun and I'd see a little Jew and he told me I had a tendency to project so maybe – do you hate me? Do you hate me? Please don't . . . it would very . . . hurtful if you hated me.

–   We've had tough times together, you and I. Let's be honest. You've bombed us. We've fought back. Tough times. There's been crossfire. The civilian casualties of war. It's been horrible. But that's all ending now.

–   It's all ending. We'll soon be on our way.

–   And you have to begin. You have to rebuild.

–   Of course there's a struggle – yes. There's nothing on a plate. But we journeyed before you. Several hundred years ago we discovered the path out of tyranny and hatred and darkness – we moved into the light and now you too can move into the light.

–   The fight was harder for us – there was no path to follow – but for you there's a path to follow – so follow, follow, follow – and all will be well.

–   There will be inward investment, there will be international recognition, there will be the freedom and light I know you crave.

–   Tomorrow my husband and I will barbecue a fish, we'll play swingball, Martin and his kids will come round. Tomorrow will be a normal day.

–   This has been a hell for us, this place. If you could see the
beauty of the place I come from and this . . . The tribal . . .
the anger, turmoil . . . This is something that will stay in my
head for a long time. I don't want to offend, but when I dream
about you they won't be good dreams. I will dream of a mission
to a city where I carried the torch of freedom but all the
people of the city wanted to do was burn me and blow me
apart and destroy the torch of freedom.

–   Not all the people. No. You are good people.

–   Of course – you are a good people.

–   But the evil people here . . .

–   You have been misled so many of you by evil people. We
have called out to you but too often evil has called out louder.

–   The convoys are ready, the air is clear. So close to goodbye.

–   Goodbye.

–   Goodbye.

Waving, music.

–   This our last gift to you. Our final gift.

*The **Dictator** is brought in.*

–   We never thought we'd find him but with Hope and
Determination anything is possible.

–   The scum.

–   You scum.

–   The lowest scum of them all.

–   A statement.

Dictator   What a sorry man I am. You saw me for thirty
years as a big man, the biggest man, but I'm not. I was greedy.
I took your money and land. I grew so big. I saw you as my
children. I wanted to love you all. But I abused you. I led you
to a nightmare. I pray for punishment.

PUNISHMENT!

My wife and sons are dead. I shot them when the city was
invaded. I wanted to protect them. I said to them, 'This is the
act of a kind man,' as I pulled the trigger. But of course it
wasn't kind. It was an act of cruelty, as all my acts have been
acts of cruelty. I pray for punishment. I was a coward. I couldn't
shoot myself. So I ran and hid in a hole in the ground.
Punishment, please.

PUNISHMENT!

But these last few months I've been in a hole in the ground.
I have had no food and now my stomach has grown so unused
to food that if I were to eat food it might kill me. I pray to the
great powers of freedom and democracy – punish me.

PUNISHMENT!

I'm a pathetic weak creature. My evil was great. I did not
believe in democracy. i did not believe in freedom. I did not
believe in choice. I did not believe in human rights. I did not
trade our oil. I did not develop our economy in the way it
should have been developed. Punish me as I should be punished.

PUNISHMENT!

Shoot me or stab me or electrocute me and hang me or throw
me from a high place. There are so many ways. I know them
all. I have used them all. You must . . .

PUNISHMENT!

I will never see the future that you will see. In twenty years'
time, you will be a fat people, shopping with joy, eating with
joy, smiling at your elected representatives, smiling as your
children debate freely at the university, trading with the world,
a world of delights – of leisure activities and entertainments.
Truly I do not deserve to see such a world.

PUNISHMENT!

I go to a hell now, the greatest hell where the darkest men in
history tear at each like dogs for all eternity. Am I frightened?

Yes, I am frightened. I am a weak, cruel man – of course I am frightened. But this is the right, this is right, this is the only thing to do.

PUNISHMENT!

The **Dictator** *kneels.*

–   Goodbye.

He is kicked to death by the **Chorus***. Throughout* –

Dictator   Thank you. Thank you. Thank you.

He dies. The male members of the **Chorus** *urinate over the corpse. Once this is done, the female members apply make-up to his face.*

–   Goodbye.

–   Goodbye.

–   Goodbye.

–   How I long for civilisation.

–   How I long for . . . ? Do you know what I long for? Breakfast. My coffee at breakfast.

–   Oh yes.

–   A really good cup of coffee. And a little pastry or – if I'm watching my figure – no little pastry. But always coffee.

–   Oh yes. And to say to the man in the pastry shop, 'Lovely weather' or 'Planning a holiday?' or 'How are the kids?' because that's what civilisation means. At the end of the day, that's what makes us civilised. Those little words as he sells me a pastry and I buy a pastry.

–   It is time to heal in my family. My little boy has been troubled. At first he was drawing pictures of people with no heads. Why? We couldn't tell. Then just one person. The soldier with no head. And then he told us the soldier with no head was coming into his room. He wet the bed. This is what war does to a child. My child. But now I'm going to play with him and there'll be theme parks and we'll go to the biggest toy warehouse and I'll say, 'Anything, anything you want,' and we'll drive home and there will be food and love. It must be possible to get over this war. I believe it must. If I didn't believe in healing, well, I wouldn't . . . I have to believe in healing.

– It was an empty relationship with my wife. I see that now. Oh, we talked all the time about the price of our house and booking for the theatre and, and, and politics and so on. But actually somehow very empty. That's all changing now. So much love from now – from now everything is love.

– Ah, the plane is ready.

– Finally we're going home.

– We're seeing home.

– At last. At last. At last. Home.

– STOP! THE BATTLE IS NOT OVER YET. STOP! THE BATTLE STILL RAGES!

– No.

– STOP! ANOTHER COUNTRY. ANOTHER COUNTRY WHICH IS THE CRADLE OF HATE. ANOTHER COUNTRY WHICH WILL DESTROY THE CIVILISED WORLD.

– No, please.

– STOP! ANOTHER COUNTRY WHERE THERE IS NO FREEDOM TO SPEAK, NO DEMOCRACY, A PLACE OF TORTURE AND FEAR.

– I want to go home please. I miss my wife so much please.

– STOP! ANOTHER COUNTRY WHICH BREAKS EVERY INTERNATIONAL AGREEMENT. ANOTHER COUNTRY TO WHOM FAIR WARNING WAS GIVEN.

– My son has a girlfriend. He's messaged me. Please, I must see my son's girlfriend at least please.

– THIS IS THE NEXT WAR. THIS IS THE NEXT INVASION. YOU WILL NOT RETURN HOME. YOU WILL INVADE. STAND BY TO INVADE.

—   Please, we are so tired, please we have to stop, please. Look.
We have lived these last few years with bombs and mines. We
lost track of who was an enemy and who was a friend. We are
so lonely. We miss our families. We miss . . . so stupid but we
miss all the tiny things about our lives, things . . . gardens,
coffee, friends, a DVD with a child. We can't go on without
these things.

—   Yes of course we believe in yes — all the core values —
freedom, democracy, yes — but we can't . . . ?

—   How long is this going on? How long?

—   The world's a strange place to us. A map frightens me.
A globe frightens me. I don't know these places. I only know
home. I want to be home.

—   How many places in the world? How many places where
they don't live as we live?

—   How many places where they don't have our core values?

—   Are there dozens of countries, scores of countries, hundreds
of countries that we have to invade?

—   We should know. We should be told. Please. Tell us. How
many countries? How many invasions? How long will this war
go on?

—   Tell us tell us tell us tell us.

—   Will this war go on and on and on and on and on and on
and on? I'm too weary, too . . .

—   We are all too weary.

—   Of course our beliefs are unshaken, yes of course our core
values, but still —

—   To sleep to sleep to sleep —

—   Just to let the world run its course — would it be so wrong
to let the world run its course?

—   We have to sleep.

Enter a small **Boy**.

Boy   I am proud of my town. I am proud of my family. I am proud of my teachers. We live a happy life. I am happy. I am learning the core values – freedom and democracy. I think they are very good.

I write to a boy in another town far away. He writes to me. He says he is sad. His father said the wrong things. Now his father has been tortured. His brain has been damaged. He can't talk to his son. He sits and looks at the wall and sometimes he cries.

My friend says: 'Who will put an end to all this suffering?'

I say: 'We should put an end to all this suffering.'

Rise up, rise up, rise up, rise up – the battle is just beginning. We are the good people and we have to bring good to the world.

You are leaving this country. You are saying goodbye. It is scarred but it will heal. Now another country calls you and then another country and then another country and then another country.

The struggle is long. The struggle is hard. But that is the future. I am the future. I'm calling you. Wake up and hear the call.

–   Please tell my wife that I love her very much. I know our marriage was often hollow but somewhere in there was love and in time . . . we would have found love. But now . . . I can't face this burden. This burden is too great. It's not that I don't believe in our core values. Of course I believe in our core values. But I can't . . . I'll take my own life. I'll leave now to take my own life. (*Leaves.*)

–   I'm ready. I know the fight is long but it must be fought if there is to be good in this world. How I envy the comfortable world of coffee and pastry but sometimes freedom and democracy demand a greater sacrifice.

–   How I long for those innocent days, innocent happy days when I thought a few years of war, a few years of war to bring freedom and democracy to a world that was hungry for freedom and democracy. How naive I was. How stupid. I'll never see my boy again. I'll never see his girlfriend. Of course I won't. Because this battle goes on forever. Take me there. I'm ready to fight again.

—   Our plane is ready. Our battle goes on. The world will have freedom and democracy.

—   Goodbye.

—   Goodbye.

Boy   That's right. That's good. It's the good thing to do. Goodbye.

Exeunt, leaving the body of the **Dictator**.

Play Sixteen

Birth of a Nation

A team of **Artist-Facilitators**.

– Your city is in ruins.

– We're being honest about – we're not trying to hide that. Your city is . . .

– A civilisation. An old civilisation is shattered.

– Eggs have been broken.

– Exactly. Exactly. Eggs have been broken. When I got off the plane, when I looked around, when I saw, I thought to myself: eggs have been broken here.

– I was met at the airport. We drove past a pile of rubble. I asked my driver: 'What's that?' And he started he cry. He cried and he said that was the university. 'That was our university. I taught in that university. For years – my students came and I encouraged them to do their very best. And now that is just brick and dust and crater.' That man, that driver, he was broken, as that building was broken.

– Everywhere it's the same, the same everywhere – craters and dust and shattered brick.

– I've never seen anything like it. You follow at home. I keep abreast on the TV but when you see it –

– Devastating.

– Shattered city.

– Shattered city and a shattered people.

– So many dead people. So many people dead because the food supplies haven't reached them. So many people dead because the food supplies have reached them and they've fallen on the food and – months of hunger – their stomachs erupt and they die. They die and they litter the streets.

—   Have you ever seen a seen a city with every building
shattered and the people shattered and the dead littering the
streets?

—   I never have.

—   Nor I.

—   Nor I.

—   Nor I. And I hope, I hope, I hope, I hope to God, it's
something I never see again. I'm looking out from my hotel
window, I'm twisting the cap on a little tiny bottle of spirits
(why am I drinking? why am I . . . ?) and I'm asking: Shit, did
we do this, did we cause all this — did we bring about this — did
we we we we we we we — did we wreak all this devastation?

—   And the answer is . . . Yes yes yes yes yes. Yes the West
came here, yes the Western powers came here, yes the Western
alliance came here, and yes our bombs, our shells, our landmines,
our soldiers, our — yes. Yes. Yes.

—   Yes and no.

—   Yes and no?

—   Yes and no, because your insurgents, your interfactional,
your tribes, your — maybe even if we hadn't, maybe if we —

—   This was a powder keg.

—   A powder keg, exactly. Exactly. Exactly. Exactly so — a
powder keg.

—   A powder keg that we — oh, what a mess. What a mess.
What a bloody fucking horrible mess.

—   What a terrible horrible fucking horrible mess these last
few years have been.

—   Fucking horrible.

—   Fucking horrible. I marched against right from the —

—   We all marched against it —

—   We all — yes — we all marched against it — right from the
beginning we marched against it, we marched against this war.

We filled the streets, we called out to stop this bloody war but still our representatives –

– Our so-called elected so-called representatives –

– – still our so-called elected so-called democratically elected so-called representatives still they went ahead and pursued their horrible bloody little war.

– Butchers.

– Butchers.

– Butchers.

– And now look what they've done to your city, to your beautiful . . . once-beautiful city.

– I've been looking you up, I looked you up and – wow! – what a culture you used to have, what a culture, what an amazing culture you used to have. Before we had a culture, before we . . . when we were sitting in mud huts in the rain, you were, you were – you had your own stories, beautiful huge really long epic stories, your alphabet, sculpting, dancing – you really – you had a culture here thousands of years ago.

– Thousands of years ago you were here asking: What is life all about? What's it all about and how should the good life be lived? What is a good life? Why do we strive for meaning on this planet? You were asking all these wonderful questions in your beautiful alphabet while we were: grunt.

– Grunt. Hunt buffalo.

– Hunt. Skin buffalo.

– Hunt. Eat buffalo.

– Yes yes yes, you were so so so far ahead of us, but now . . .

– But now . . .

– But now . . .

– What a horrible sight to see a world blown apart like this, but still –

–   But still –

–   But still –

–   The army's gone now, the army's withdrawing, the army's just . . . Only the peacekeeping force remaining so . . . Calm is returning.

–   Calm is here.

–   Here is calm. Here is . . . a time to rebuild, a time to heal, a time to . . . regroup, rebuild, heal . . . a new forward.

–   A time to move forward.

–   Move forward. Which is why, which is why, that's why we're here. Hello.

–   Hello.

–   Hello. Hi. Hi. Hi.

–   Hi. We're artists. We're a group of – that's what we all do – we're all artists.

–   I'm a painter. I paint.

–   I'm a writer. I write.

–   I'm a dancer. I dance.

–   And I . . . I do a sort of art performance installation sort of bonkers thing.

–   Oh yes, oh yes. And what we do is, what we do, we come to a place like this, a place like this where there's been the most terrible pain and horror and there's . . . We come to a place where everyone's been hurting and we start the healing process by working through, by working with art.

–   We'd like to work with you. Work with you. With art.

–   No, listen, okay, no listen, right, bear with us, okay? Just bear with us, alright? This works, alright? This works. This totally works. We know what we're doing.

–   We've just come from the most horrendous civil war, the most terrible . . . The country was divided in two, neighbour against neighbour, brother against sister, a husband turning on his own wife and stabbing her in the night – and we spent months there and eventually if you . . . people tell stories, people, they paint, they come together . . . they perform together . . . And eventually if you really work at it, if people really listen, if people then eventually . . . peace does return. Peace does come back. People aren't naturally animals. People don't naturally tear at each other like animals. People naturally rub along. If you allow them to, they rub along. And that's what we do, through art, we allow them to rub along.

–   I was a miner. I was born a miner. There'd been mines in my region for centuries. Every man in my family had gone down the mine for as long as anyone could remember. Every morning, you got up at six and you marched with all the other men and you reached the pithead and you put a helmet on and you collected your pick and you were lowered into the shaft and sixteen hours later you came home. And some men were – excuse me – cunts and beat their wives and got drunk and some men were sober and went to chapel and played in the band or sang in the choir on a Sunday. And that was life. For hundreds of years that was life. Then one day, we came through the town to find a sign: 'Pit closed'. Pit closed. Pit closed. Every pit in our region closed. Every pit in, every job practically in our region gone overnight. What a blow. You just . . . your world is gone. We did fight. Of course we fought. The union. But . . . the bosses, government, big business and big government – so much stronger than the people, so much stronger than a few thousand miners. But also stronger because I think – can I be honest, can I be totally honest here?

–   Please.

–   Please.

–   Please.

–   I think in our hearts we knew – I've never said this before – we knew, yes, we were fighting for a community, a way of life, the dignity of blah, yes – but we were fighting for the right to be shut away in the dark, shut down in the pit and have the coal on our lungs and the right to die an early death and that was . . .

– I marched alongside you then. I was only a student, but we skipped our studies and we jumped in a car and we drove down to your region and we marched alongside you: 'Keep the mine open, keep the mine open.'

– And thanks for that, I am grateful for that, but still you . . . protesting for – the right for that terrible hacking death was . . . in our gut, we knew that . . . we knew what a pointless fight that was, but still when the pit closed, when the jobs finished. So many people . . .

– Suicide? Heroin? Depression?

– Yes yes yes. Suicide heroin depression. You look at the places, the places where there's everything, where there's jobs and life and money and your world is – so quickly your world becomes suicide heroin depression.

– For me it was abuse. The terrible abuse I'd suffered as a child. My father had . . . I couldn't see any way of moving forward but . . .

– All I could hope for was that the mine would open again. How stupid was that? I mean, how fucking stupid was that? That was fucking stupid. Wasn't it?

– Was it?

– Oh yes. That was totally fucking stupid. The mine wasn't going to open, really I shouldn't even want it to open – in a sane world – but still, when you can't see a way forward . . .

– Heal through Art. I saw the sign at the hospital. I'd had no help from the doctor. I'd practically screamed at him: 'My father fucking raped me you cunt help me help me help help me I'm in pain all day long. I'm in pain all day long,' but he'd done nothing about it and then I saw the sign: 'Heal Through Art'. And I thought, Why not? Why not? I was at my lowest ebb. And so I went to the meeting and there was the paints and there was Lynne and Lynne just said: 'Use the paints, use

the paints and let it all out, let it all out however you will.' And
I did. I let it out. I let it out.

—   A dance workshop. I was . . . I was just . . . I thought it was
stupid. I was pissed up at home – that's all I'd do those days –
get pissed up from tins and wank with videos – piss and a
wank – when Hannah came round and said we're doing a
dance workshop. And I was like, fuck off fuck off.

—   We found . . . black people and white people, there was so
much distrust, so much history, just to be in a room together,
and when John asked me to pair up with this guy and write a
play together – a short little play – I was like, 'Oh my God, I
can't believe this is happening, our skin is different colours and
here we are sitting down and writing this little play together.'
I mean – I wouldn't have shared a bus with this guy and here
we are writing a play together.

—   My father. His face. His penis. The blood pouring from
me. Over and over again I painted it, over and over again, and
Lynne didn't comment, Lynne didn't – she was brilliant, Lynne
was brilliant – Lynne was just like: 'Keep going. Wonderful. Be
brave. Keep going.'

—   But eventually something . . . I think maybe the fact that
Hannah was German and the German girls on the video were
always the filthiest girls – something made me go to Hannah's
dance workshop. And fuck me – there was loads of my mates
from the mine.

—   I suppose you know . . . socialism was so important to me,
Marxism was . . . I was a Marxist . . . That was . . . that was
my yardstick and then when that all, that sort of imploded . . .
then suddenly I was sort of cast into darkness . . . It was one
of those real, you know, 'Father Father why have you forsaken
me?' moments. And without Marxism this world was suddenly
a pretty fucking pointless fucking place, you know. And so what
I was looking for, I suppose, what I was looking for was a form
in which I could express that sense of . . . I don't know . . .
that essential formlessness, the weightlessness, the dizzying lack
of gravity in a state of fallen . . . And that's when I discovered

the whole performance art installation bonkers sort of thing, you know, and that really seemed to, seemed to, seemed to give meaning to the lack of meaning – if that makes any sense.

–   And it wasn't dance, like – it wasn't ballet, okay? It wasn't tutus and all that shit. It was taking the gestures, the bodies, the gestures and the bodies of ordinary men and women and creating a whole new language from that, a language of theatre, which we . . . And now people come, they come from miles, they drive from the financial towns and the centres of government and commerce and they come to our old mining region and they stay in the new fabulous hotels and they eat in the new fabulous restaurants and the new fabulous hotels and they watch us dance, they watch the fabulous pieces of dance theatre that Hannah has created. And now our region has a new life. Mining wasn't us. That was our definition. But actually that was our prison and now . . .

–   I'm not in this to sell my work. Am I a Vermeer? Am I a Manet? Am I a Bacon? I don't know. I don't know and I don't care. This is about me. This is about me healing. And I have, I have healed. I acknowledge what happened in the past. I acknowledge what was done to that poor little frightened little child – to me – I acknowledge that and now I . . . any time I feel bad about myself – out come the paints and splosh! The healing begins. And now I've started to – one week Lynne said: 'I can't make it next week, and will you lead the group?' And I was – ooooh! But actually, you know actually, you know actually, you know I loved it and I still love it. I'm still loving it to this day.

–   Extraordinary plays I've seen written all over the world. I bring people together in clusters – bring enemies together to write dialogue and we're creating – Oh it's wonderful, it's wonderful, it's wonderful, I love it, I love, I love, I love, I love, I love it.

–   There's so much work to do here. There is so much pain to heal. There is so much anger that is burning brightly.

–   We acknowledge that.

–   We see that. We really do.

–   But you must sign up for the dance or the writing or the painting or the performance installation workshops.

–   You must.

–   You must.

–   You must do it.

–   Look, I don't want to be heavy-handed about this, but you have to . . . You want inward investment? You want tourism? You want civilisation? You want freedom and democracy ? You want all – and if this war hasn't been about . . . then what has it been about? – you want all that then let some culture in, sign up for some culture, embrace some culture, let some culture into the ruins of this shattered city – your city lives.

–   Look – why?

–   Why aren't you painting?

–   Why aren't you dancing?

–   Writing.

–   Art performance installation bonkers thing.

–   Come on, you bastards, you fucking ungrateful, you fucking –

–   This is art, you bastards, this is art, this is fucking art, everybody likes art, everybody wants art, so make some fucking art.

–   Wouldn't it be great? Wouldn't it be great? Wouldn't it be great in a few years' time if this was a city of culture, if this city had a festival like . . . other cities have festivals, decent cities have festivals, cities with . . . opera and art and theatre and jugglers and sponsors and beer tents and – it's like a rebirth, these places are reborn, with the arts these places are reborn.

–   As we want you to be reborn.

–   As we want you to be reborn.

—   With a wonderful festival of all the wonderful arts your city can be reborn.

—   Your city will be reborn.

—   Because we want – and you want it – your city will be reborn.

—   Who's coming forward? Who's coming forward? Let's have some come forward so that the healing can begin.

—   The healing power of art can begin.

A **Blind Woman** *is brought forward.*

—   Our first artist.

—   Our first artist.

—   Hurrah!

—   Hurrah!

—   Hurrah!

—   Tell us your story – please tell us of your pain and struggle so the art can be made and the healing can begin.

The **Blind Woman** *opens her mouth. Blood pours out.*

—   The woman has no tongue.

—   This woman has lost her tongue and she has lost her eyes.

—   It has been a hard war.

—   It has been a bitter war.

—   There is a terrible price to pay to win freedom and democracy.

The **Blind Woman** *grunts, holds out a photo, gesticulates.*

—   This woman has lost her family. She has no family. She has no eyes and no tongue and no family. We can only imagine how deeply your pain must run.

—   But still you can paint. Here. (*Gives her a brush.*)

– But still you can write. Here. (*Gives her a pen.*)

– Still you can dance the dance of the gestures of the people. (*Her body is moved.*)

– Join me in an installation. Come come come.

– It's beginning. You see – it's beginning. The darkness is ending, the darkness is ending and light and civilisation and democracy and art are moving forward – once again they are moving forward, once again –

The **Blind Woman** *screams, throws pen and brush away.*

– That's it, be brave. Express. Create. Be bold.

The **Blind Woman** *screams.*

– It's happening, it's happening, it's happening.

The **Blind Woman** *convulses, her body in spasms.*

– Oh yes dance dance dance.

The **Blind Woman** *spasms, the* **Chorus** *applaud, lights fade to black.*

Appendix

Yesterday an Incident Occurred

Although originally written as part of the play cycle, Yesterday an Incident Occurred *was substantially adapted for BBC Radio 3.*

Sound of the live audience coming into the hall.

A   Good evening.

B   Tonight a nation gathers. Hurrah!

C   Tonight some of you are here with us in person. Hello – people.

A   Good. Good. Welcome to you. Welcome to this great hall. The hall where our city's democracy swings into action. Take your seats.

B   Some of you are not here with us but in your homes. In the homes you own and care for. And you are joining us on transistor and broadband and Freeview and laptop. Welcome and hurrah!

A   And you are listening not only here but around the world. Hurrah! For just as our freedom and our democracy spreads throughout the globe bringing peace and prosperity, so does our broadcasting spread throughout the globe, bringing peace and prosperity wherever it goes. For wherever transistor and podcast and broadband go, so there will justice surely follow.

A/B/C   Hurrah! Hurrah! Hurrah!

C   Now some of you may not own property, some of you may have done nothing but the most meagre shopping this weekend – you may have envied the rest of us our trip to the garden centre and thought: if only I owned a garden, if only I could buy a bench. But we are inclusive and you, the poor and downtrodden and lonely and illiterate, can join us here. No group, however much they are in a minority, is excluded here. Always room at the back in a multimedia democratic

broadcasting environment. Hurrah! Any people here want to – ?
Ah. Here's a person. A man in a yellow tie. Hello.

One (*pushes forward*)   Me. Me. I'm here. I'm here because . . .
well, because . . . I live in this city and I think it's a lovely city
Not just the shops of course – although the shops are lovely,
we have lovely shops. But also we have lovely culture. We are a
city of culture. And we're proud of that. And there's a choice
of culture, a great deal of choice of – an overwhelming choice
of culture. Later I may look at some culture. Maybe I'll take in
the Vermeer. There's fireworks promised in the park tonight
and – wonderful! – next week a whole week of Monteverdi.
That's a sure sign you're in a lovely city of culture when they
play Monteverdi. So why not join us here any time in our city
of culture? I'm here for the announcement the – I support the
authorities – justice and democracy – freedom and light – / a
choice of broadcast media in a digital –

C   Good, good. To your seat. Please.

One (*retreats*)   I believe I believe. / Justice and democracy.

C   Yes. You're a person. We are people. Here are people.
Hurrah! Hurrah for you!

B   And so. Our nation gathers together here because now
we, the speakers, have an important announcement to make.
So . . . settle please – audience with us here, settle.

Take out noise of live audience arriving.

Audience around the nation, globe – settle. Thank you. Good
evening. We have an announcement. To make.

A   We do. An announcement. About civilisation and barbarity.

B   An announcement. About innocence and guilt.

C   An announcement. About the normal and the unforgivable.

B   About the ordinary citizen and the part that he, she, that
you can and must play in keeping our society free from the
forces of barbarity and terror.

A   You here with us – and you with your meal or your child or your washing in your home – you must join us now at this time of crisis in stopping the terror in our society.

C   Do you agree with us?

B   Please agree with us. Do you agree with us?

One   I agree with you.

C   Who's that? Oh. Man in the yellow tie. You agree with us? You all agree with us?

One   Totally.

C   Good. Good. Good.

B   That's important. Because yesterday, you see, yesterday an incident occurred.

C   Yesterday an incident occurred of a violent nature.

B   Yesterday a . . .

A   CCTV footage of the incident is available to you at home. It's available as a video download now. Click your mouse now on 'brutal attack' for the video download. You can follow the horrific CCTV footage. Are you doing that? Please do that now. Click now.

We now hear the footage running on plasma screens in the hall.

B   Meanwhile here we are showing yesterday's brutal attack to our invited audience. We are showing the brutal attack now to the people with us here on our plasma screens. They are horrific images. The people here are – How do you feel about these horrible images? Let's go to . . . Anyone? Man in the yellow tie?

One   I'm nervous and and . . . revolted.

B   Nervous and revolted by these sickening images?

One   Nervous and revolted by these sickening images. As your listeners at homes will be nervous and revolted –

B   – if they download now.

A   If your computer does not have the correct software (why?) or if poverty or disability exclude you from viewing the podcast vid clip download, here's an audio description – inclusion, inclusion, inclusion, democracy, democracy, democracy – of the incident that occurred yesterday. Someone describe . . .

C   But please – a warning – it's a violent and sickening incident. Totally sickening. Who will describe what's happening on the screen?

One   Me.

C   Again? – Man in the yellow tie. Very well. Describe. What do you see?

One   The incident takes place in the shopping centre. The shopping centre where every normal man and woman goes every day to do the thing that the human animal does most naturally, to shop. It's a bright day. And here's a man – see him? – a man . . .

C   He's called Alan and he's with his wife and she's called Marion. Very much in love. Thirty years married but very much in love. See that on the footage which the security forces have made public? Alan turns to Marion and he says – the cameras picked this up – sound right up please . . .

Alan (*very muffled*)   I love you.

One   'I love you. I love you. I love you.' We should all remember that. Alan is reaching out to buy a purple sweater.

C   He and Marion have talked about it all week and now they feel, now is the time for a purple sweater.

One   Alan lets go of Marion's devoted hand for a moment to open the door of the shop where the purple sweaters are sold and . . . we switch cameras, and they are inside the shop.

C   This is the only reassuring thing in this otherwise disturbing footage.

One   Oh yes. To know we are watched always is our only comfort in this world.

New muffled acoustic: the shop, muzak.

But now as Alan reaches for the purple sweater a man leaps from the crowd – a stranger, an unprovoked . . . just leaps and throws Alan to the ground.

We hear all this on the very bad CCTV mike.

The man is tearing at Alan and kicking him. Marion is trying to pull him off.

Marion (*muffled*)   No no off off help.

One   And now the attacker is screaming – well . . .

C   Listen hard, see if you can make out the words.

Attacker (*very, very muffled, almost impossible to make out*)   I hate you. I hate everything about your world. I hate it.

C   Almost impossible to make out the words, yes? But we used lip-readers and sound engineers – took off the bottom, fiddled with the top – and we reconstructed a text. And here's what we believe the attacker was saying when he leapt from the crowd and attacked – totally unprovoked – attacked Alan. Here's – please, man in the yellow tie.

One   'I hate you. I hate everything about your world. I hate it.'

C   'I hate you. I hate everything about your world. I hate it.' Chilling words. A horrible attack. The video clip ends.

Silence. Pause.

A   How does that make you feel? You here with us? You at home? How does yesterday's terrible incident make you feel? That unprovoked attack on Alan.

B   Were you affected by the podcast, the video screens or the audio decription? If you were, seek professional help and appropriate medication today. Or call us now and share your feelings, call or text or email us now to tell us what you feel. We want to know. We're a democratic broadcaster in a multimedia enviroment. We all have feelings. Feelings are

everything. And in this democracy your feelings are everything.
How do you feel? The lines are open now.

C   Let's ask somebody here with us in the live audience –
let's ask them how they feel about that sickening disgusting
attack. Yes – you – how do you feel about the attack? Man
in the yellow tie.

One   Well . . . Sickened. Disgusted. Angry.

C   Angry?

One   Yeah, angry, angry, and, and, very very sad. I want to
say: they are cancer. These attackers. They are the scumming
cancer dregs. That's what I want to say. And we shouldn't have
to take it. We shouldn't – the ordinary men and women.
Terror – random, violent, horrible, random, pointless attacks.
There is a war on. Abroad. At home. Right here. No one is
safe. If people can just leap from the crowd – they leap and
they assault another human being and they just batter him.
Batter him to death. It's quite horrible.

A   Well, thank you, let's –

One   I don't remember this from childhood. Did people just
leap from the crowd and batter you to death when I was a
child? I don't think so, I don't think so. Oh no. But there are
normal things.

A   Thank you, if we –

One   There's still normality. Oh yes. I had a lovely day
yesterday. Yesterday I walked by the river. It was a beautiful
day. I watched some planes overhead. Some of our brave boys
and girls practising for the battle ahead, and I thought: This
is perfect, this is lovely, this is the most perfect day of my life.
And I – I remember now – I ate linguine in the evening. Oh
yes, linguine – Sorry I don't want to . . .

A   Please – your contributions are valuable. You are an ideal
figure to pick from the crowd.

One   Alright. I just wanna . . . yeah . . . I just wanna say:
Most of us are ordinary. And let's not forget that. Let's not

forget to celebrate the wonderful, ordinary men and women.
The backbone. The backbone should be celebrated. We should
be celebrating the men and women who get up in the morning,
get up, drink their coffee for breakfast, then do their bit – do
their bit to generate wealth for the ordinary families that make
up this society. And tonight those families will be sitting down
and sharing some lovely meals together after another normal
day. Not this terrorist, cancer, scum, dregs. We hear enough
about the terrorist, cancer, scum, dregs. Let's hear more about
the ordinary men and women.

A/B/C   Hurrah! Hurrah! Hurrah!

Applause.

B   Let's go – we've got a reporter at the hospital – let's go
over to the hospital.

One   Oh yes. How's Alan doing after yesterday's sickening
disgusting unprovoked attack that has left us all feeling angry
and sad?

Reporter (*busy hospital acoustic*)   Alan's in a bad way. Alan's in
a very bad way. Marion is by his bed. Doctors are describing
his condition as critical. A lung has been punctured. There's
bleeding on the brain. Will Alan pull through after yesterday's
sickening disgusting unprovoked attack that has left us all
feeling angry and sad? Those are the words on everyone's lips
here: 'Can Alan pull through?' (*Commotion, flashbulbs.*) I can see
Marion – there's Marion – Marion, can Alan pull through?

Marion (*slightly off mike*)   All we can do is hope and pray.
He's a civilised, decent . . . he's my rock. And the scum who
did this, this scum will . . .

The line goes down.

B   We've lost them. We'll get them back.

C   Let's hope – he's a civilised, decent, normal human being –
let's hope Alan pulls through.

B   Wait. My producer's passed me a note. He's been caught –
a man we believe to be the attacker has been caught. If you

here look now at the plasma screens – or you at home, a ten-second clip is available now as a download if you text CANCER SCUM straight away – the footage, the footage of the face of, the face that we're already calling the face of evil. What would you like us to do with this man?

A   What would you like us to do with this attacker? Call us.

B   Press your red button now. It's on your remote at home.

A   What do you think should happen to the face of evil?

C   Maybe we should remind ourselves of his words as reconstructed by our experts. Maybe someone can read them – erm – yes – you read them again, man in the yellow tie.

One (*reads*)   'I hate you. I hate everything about your world. I hate it.'

C   Chilling words. A terrible attack. The face of evil. And now – we believe – apprehended.

B   Man in the yellow tie. What would you do the face of evil?

One   Kill him.

B   Really? Kill him? Really?

One   Oh yes – really kill him.

A   Kill him? Yes? Yes? Yes?

B   And the red buttons have been pressed. A nation has spoken. Democracy. What are the results?

C   Well . . . red buttons have been pressed and then – oh democracy and justice – the overwhelming majority of you joining us from home and overseas agree. Just listen to these voices from a selection of callers.

Callers (*montage*)   Kill him. Kill him. Kill him. Kill him. Kill him.

B   Listen. We would like to kill him. We really would like to. But there is justice. There are systems. Checks and balances. The liberals. You understand.

A   We will kill him if we . . . We only believe it was this man –
his face, you see, is partially obscured? Run the CCTV . . .

Muffled noise of the CCTV footage.

The angle, his face isn't entirely clear – you see? You see?
Thank you. End the CCTV footage.

CCTV footage ends.

B   So – we need a witness.

C   Yes. A witness is needed.

B   Yesterday an incident took place of a violent nature and
a witness is needed.

A   We are here today to announce to you the nation –

B   A proud nation of multimedia choices in a democratic
age –

C   We are here to announce to you that a witness is needed.
Yesterday an incident occurred. We have caught the probable
attacker. And we want to kill him. You want to kill him. But –
please – we need a witness.

A   Is that witness you? Is it you, man or woman, sat here with
us tonight in the audience? Did you witness yesterday's brutal
attack? If you did you must come forward.

Pause.

B   Come on. Someone saw the attack.

C   Or was it you listening on your couch or bed or in your
garage at home? Was it you – yes, you at home there with your
transistor by your bed or laptop in the study – or you with
your stereo in the car? Did you witness yesterday's attack? If
you did – come forward.

A   Step forward. Call the helplines. Press the red button.
Make yourself known to the authorities. Please.

C   'I am a witness.' Those are all the words you need. You
will be treated fairly.

B   But remember this. It is your responsibility. Because you have, oh yes, not just rights but responsibilities in this shining land of democracy.

C   Come forward.

B   Come forward.

A   Come forward now.

Pause.

No? No? No? NO! NOBODY?

B   Listen, we don't want to get heavy – sorry sorry sorry – but it is an offence, it is an offence to witness a violent assault and not report it to the authorities. COME FORWARD.

C   Or . . . you will be punished. PUNISHED. Remember remember remember that it is a punishable offence to witness a brutal attack and not come forward.

Pause.

A   Alright, alright. You were given your warning. One of you is a witness. We know that. The outcome of this broadcast is inevitable because we know that one of you witnessed the attack, has not come forward and must be punished. Someone listening at home – or in maybe you, our live audience – one of you is that witness. So here's what we're going to do. We are currently assessing your level of guilt. You here in the audience. But also you at home. We have so much information. There is CCTV footage, there is search-engine usage, there is credit- and debit-card purchasing, there is travel-card use. We are using all this data and so much more and you will be graded on a scale of innocence to guilt, clean to dirt, health to cancerous scum. The information is in the computer. The computer is grading the reports. Now. Sit back and let the computer find the guilty. Run the computer.

One   Alright. Stop. Enough. Enough. Please stop. Listen. Listen. Listen. Listen. It's me. I'm the witness. The man in the yellow tie. I witnessed the brutal attack. Alan. The purple jumper. I didn't come forward.

C   You? Really? Man in the yellow tie?

B   Yes – man in the yellow tie. You scum.

One   Yes. I am. I am scum. Yesterday an incident took place and I watched the incident. I watched the incident. Yesterday. I witnessed and then I walked away. That was me. I witnessed an incident and I did not come forward, I did not confess, I . . . I knew the rules but still I did not come forward. Why did I do that? Why? I don't know. I remember that taking place but – how to say this? – I remember it happening to another person, another city, another time. An incident occurred and I was a witness and yet – somehow – not a witness. I was there but somehow . . .

B   So . . . you are guilty?

One   Am I guilty? I . . . Yes. I'm utterly guilty.

C   Don't just sit there with the ordinary men and women. Stand up. Step out of the crowd.

One   I am a guilty one. That's what drew me here tonight. I was drawn here tonight because I am guilty scum and I seek punishment.

C   Bring him forward. Come forward. Scum. What should we do with guilty people like you, I wonder? Well?

One   How would you punish me? Well –

C   I'd like to know what you think, listener to a democratic broadcaster in a multimedia age. Text or email us now.

One   What should the punishment be for me?

C   Oh! The first emails and texts are arriving already. They're coming in thick and fast. You've been emailing and texting us in vast numbers to tell us what to do with guilty people who witness and don't come forward.

A   I'm looking through the pile (*massive paper rustle*) and 'Kill the cancer scum' comes the cry. What do you think of that, eh, man in the yellow tie?

One   It's . . . appropriate. Totally, yes. Hang and disembowel. Please.

C   Exactly. Appropriate. Something has to be done. Something. Yesterday's was just the latest in a string of unprovoked barbaric attacks.

One   And ever since these unprovoked sickening attacks began it was clear that new measures would be needed. New times, new crimes, new measures. Harsher times crush forgiveness and demand punishment.

A   New punishments that take account of the new terrible age we live in.

One   Please. Punish me. Kill me. Give me satisfaction. I beg the nation.

B   I'm getting a message from my producer. Oh! – interesting – a committee has been meeting to consider the new forms of punishment needed in this new age of terror. Fantastic news. Have we got a link? Does anyone know?

C   Have we? Can anyone . . . ? Yes Yes. We have we have. We've got a link. A little shaky down the line but basically . . .

B   Great. Let's join them. Then let's join them now. Let's join the committee live as they decide how to punish those like you who witness an attack and don't come forward.

New acoustic. A committee meeting.

Chair   A range of options to punish the rotten eggs in a democractic and humane society. To punish those who witness the attacks, who witness the attacks but do not come forward. And after questioning witnesses and balancing investment and projected incomes, we have concluded that branding – branding is the way ahead. Now if you look at the video screen you'll see an example of a branding. Can we have the video screen?

Off, on the video: the sound of chatter between guards and a prisoner.

Thank you. There will be branding you with an iron. If found guilty the accused will be – At the moment it's illegal of course.

But this is a branding that took place in a – shall we say? – sympathetic – yes – a sympathetic neighbouring country whose laws are more . . . they are more . . . clarified than our own. Now if you look you can see . . . The iron will be heated to 250 degrees centigrade prior to the branding. And then . . .

Murmurs of approval.

So if you watch now you will see – yes – here is the branding. Watch the screen to see an example of a perfect branding.

From the screen, the muffled struggle of the prisoner, the guards calling 'Hold him down' and then finally the sizzle of the flesh.

Murmurs from the committee.

And there you have it. The perfect branding. It is necessary to do these things if we are to live in a civilised society. A society where rights are matched by responsibilities. I am convinced – convinced – that all decent citizens will join us in welcoming the branding of those who do not come forward.

Questioner   Mr Chairman, a question – will there be scarring?

Chair   Oh yes. Just here. Just above the right elbow. A livid scar will remain just above the right elbow for life.

Murmurs of on the whole approval but some discomfort.

In the report, a third of the study group actually – oh, bit of a surprise – thanked us for the branding.

Murmurs.

I would like to propose we pass this recommendation straight away to our elected representatives. A recommendation to make branding legal. Are we agreed? A show of hands.

All   Agreed!

Chair   Excellent. The bill will go before our elected representatives straight away. The emergency powers.

The link ends.

B   Well – there we have it, branding. Branding. How do you feel about that, man in the yellow tie?

One   I think it's brilliant.

B   Let's link up with Marion. Marion is the wife' of the man who was assaulted yesterday outside the coffee shop in the city centre. Marion's on a link from the bedside of her critically ill husband. Good evening, Marion. You've got a message for the man in the yellow tie and for the world.

Marion (*link, hospital acoustic*)   I have.

A   Will you read it to us, Marion? Would you like to do that?

Marion   I certainly would.

Judge   Then – please . . .

Marion   'Please punish this man who witnessed and did not report this terrible assault upon my husband. He is my rock. I have been married to him for twenty years and in all that time he has been a rock. He has never done anything but good in this world. He loves life and treasures everything about the freedom and democracy we enjoy. This morning, as I brought him a cup of coffee, to his bedside in the hospital, he held out his hand to me and said the words: "I love you." This is my hope. In all the middle of so much evil, love will always continue. I know I've spoken to my elected representative and asked her to ensure the new branding measure is passed without delay and I hope anyone listening to this will do the same. Freedom must triumph. Democracy must triumph. I want these rotten eggs branded. I say it on my website, I'm blogging it to the world, and please I'm sending this message to listeners at home and abroad, on digital and broadband: brand them, brand them, brand them.'

A   Thank you, Marion. A very clear voice. An admirably clear voice. You see, man in the yellow tie?

One   Yes. Yes. It's the voice of the people and it's righteously raised in anger. Hurrah!

A/B/C   Hurrah! Hurrah! Hurrah!

One   Can I ask that you say a prayer here with me? And you listening at home, please join me. Stop what you're doing. Stop and get down on your knees. A prayer – doesn't matter if you're not religious – can I ask that you join me? A prayer that the voice of the people be heard in the house of our elected representatives and that my branding be made legal.

Murmurs of agreement.

Let us pray. O Lord, I thank you for your normal world. I thank you for the normal men and normal women who move about this normal city. I thank you for the normal cultural and normal leisure activities I enjoy on this normal day. Blessed be the normal coffee I drink.

Response   Blessed be the coffee that we drink.

One   Blessed be the normal breakfast roll I break and enjoy each morning.

Response   Blessed be our breakfast roll.

One   Blessed be my Vermeer and Monteverdi, the jugglers and the comedians, the *Bacchae* of Euripides and the wonderful drama – the drama I enjoy on film, on television, theatre and the radios that inhabit thy earth. Give me this day an excellent rate of interest. Blessed be this loyalty card. In mall and in retail outlet, online and instore. And cursed be the . . . the the . . . oh . . . the . . . Cursed be the rotten eggs such as me, those who witness the attacks and do not come forward. Curse them as you once cursed Lucifer and the rebel army as you threw them into Hell. O Lord, send wisdom to our elected representatives. Send our elected representatives the wisdom to pass this legislation. This legislation which will allow those here to brand me.

Response   Brand him.

One   Brand me forever and evermore. Amen.

All   Hallelujah. Amen.

One   It will come, it must come, that day must surely come. When I shall be branded. Then there will be justice and music and dancing and champagne. And oh, how happy our world will be. A blessed place, A good place. A calm place. A happy place. It's so close. It's just a, a, a – a breath. Yes. It's just a breath away.

B   Thank you, man in the yellow tie. Please, we have to brand people. We have to. It's the only option. It's the only option under the circumstances. You listening at home: who is your representative? Who are they? Will you be calling them, texting them, emailing them – today? Do it today – you must, you must, you must, you must, you must. Democracy is there for you to make use of. Make use of democracy. Let's hear what the backbone has to say. We may lose it, we may lose it. Don't take it for granted. If you don't text or email now and call out for branding, democracy may wither away. Just wither away. And die. Democracy will be dead. It's up to you in the live audience and you at home. Do you love democracy? Or do you hate democracy? Which is it going to be? Contact your representative now. Just text the words BRAND HIM now.

C   Look – look – look at the screens.

Sound of a debate on a TV screen and under.

Reporter   Hello. I'm at the House of Representatives. It's starting. Our elected representatives are meeting. A special meeting of the House of Representatives has been called in the light of yesterday's attack. The engine of democracy has swung into action. They're debating a bill to allow branding to take place.

B   But will the branding be in public? Will it be carried on prime time?

Reporter   Well, I understand here's an advertising lobby for it to be carried on prime time. Will it be a ticketed event? The Culture Minister says yes. Will medical and legal supervision be thorough? Or even excessive? Or maybe the liberals will, maybe they'll chip away with their 'amendments'.

B   As is their right.

Reporter   As is their right. In a democracy. Let's wait and see, shall we? Let's wait and see. But democracy is taking its course. Democracy and freedom and hope and truth.

TV screen off.

A   Let's question this man in the yellow tie. And who knows, maybe by the time the trial is finished the law for branding will be in place?

One   I sincerely hope so. We must punish wrongdoers. I'm a wrongdoer. I must be branded.

A   I'm not sure if I've got the stomach for it. Wielding an iron. Flesh.

B   Nor I.

C   Nor I.

A   You see, I've planned a day of relaxing activities. I've planned a day of incredibly soothing activities. This is . . .
I love this city. It's a wonderful city. It's bristling with culture.
There's comedy and opera and jugglers and – ooh – oratoria.
And it's my belief we should – what's the . . . ? – revel! We should revel in that. Yes? Yes? Yes? Maybe I won't brand

B   I think, at heart, we're liberals.

C   I am – oh yes – at heart – a liberal.

One   Oh no. Not after everything – no no no. You must brand me. You must. The iron here –

A   It's barbaric.

One   It's right. Do you believe in cameras?

A   Of course I –

One   There were of course cameras yesterday when the incident occurred. CCTV. And it will assist us to finally confirm that I witnessed the assault and failed to come forward. I've always supported the cameras. I would visit garden centres.
I would wake to the smell of coffee and croissants prepared by the girl and I would say to my beautiful wife – I have a beautiful wife – 'I think a visit to the garden centre this morning.' And would I mind if a camera was watching?
Would I object to observation and analysis? Clearly not.

Clearly not. I would have a camera in my car, a camera in
the petrol station, a camera in the quiet corner where I chose
my garden bench if I could. And I would have them there
happily, I would . . . I would . . .

A   Embrace?

One   Embrace them. Because here in my heart of hearts,
here in my soul, in my gut, in my head, I am guilty, I am evil,
I am scum, I am cancer, oh, I am cancer scum. I must be
watched by the normal people. Because you are the normal
people and you must watch and identify and crush and then –
oh, how we'll . . . The time is coming, it's coming now, when
us scum will be wiped away and only you the backbone will be
left. Oh yes. Hallelujah!

A/B/C   Hallelujah!

One   O Lord O Lord O my God my Father my God thy
world will be cleansed. It shall, it shall, it shall. Just as thy
Heaven was made free from the sinful ones, just as you cast
Lucifer down, so shall this city, our country, our empire be
clean, clean, clean, clean. So shall I be branded.

One *begins to sob.*

C   That's it, that's it. Act normally. I'm a liberal, I believe
everyone should act normally. Smile or frown or . . . cry. Yes,
you can cry if you want to. Sob. Whatever you feel is
appropriate. That's it. I empathise.

One   What?

C   I'm feeling what you're –

One   You musn't. Look at the CCTV footage. I'll describe.

Muffled sound of footage.

I'll tell you what I see. I see a man who . . . it is myself. Yes. It's
me – scum – and I'm . . . A cup of coffee arrives. I drink the
coffee. I have a pastry. I read a listings magazine. I suppose I'm
considering, yes, considering the possibilities for cultural, for
cultural or for leisure activities in this great city. And now I go

into a shop because I want to buy a yellow tie. It's my birthday
and . . . Now . . . a member of the public steps forward, steps
forward out of his – it's a man – steps forward and – oh –
strikes one of the shoppers about the head. And now that poor
innocent shopper falls to the floor. And the man – the attacker,
the face of evil – is kicking him in a frenzy of, kicking him . . .
bones are broken, there is severe bruising, bleeding. The skull
is fractured. Another man steps forward from the crowd and
tries to pull the attacker off. But the attacker is frenzied. He's
lost his mind. He is overcome with anger and he pours it into
the poor broken body of that poor shopper.

A　You are watching and listening?

One　Yes. I am. 'I hate you. Everything about you. Your
world.' I hear that clearly. So, please, you mustn't feel anything
for me.

C　I'll do my best.

B　We're getting news – we've got some news. On the link.

A　Then – feed it through.

Reporter (*hospital acoustic*)　Bad bad bad bad tragic bad news.
Sorry to say – that. I'm with Marion and a family friend –

Friend　Hello.

Reporter　– and . . . please tell us, Marion.

Marion　I . . . I . . . I can't . . .

Friend　I'm a family friend. I'll say it for you, Marion.
Marion's husband has just died.

Reporter　Really?

Friend　Really. His internal injuries. Very severe internal
injuries. Injuries sustained during the brutal assault yesterday
in . . . I'm sorry, Marion, I can't, a moment . . . I . . . Oh my
Lord. (*Sobs.*)

Marion　What is it? Come on, come on.

Friend　I spent – one summer – I never told you, Marion,
but one summer . . .

Marion   Yes?

Friend   We were lovers that summer. Before you – Marion . . . We spent the summer on a boat drifting across a lake making love under the moon and stars. We read Shakespeare. *The Winter's Tale.* It was so beautiful. We had such a bond. Oh, this is hurting me very very very very deeply. Medication, counselling, what do I do?

A   How do you feel about that? I ask the accused with us here.

One   . . . I'm incredibly saddened by the unnecessary death of a fellow human being. I am almost inconsolable. Words cannot express the grief that any of us feel for that man's death. Please give me the very harshest punishment.

Marion (*hospital*)   Please, I – Can you still hear me?

A   We can hear you, Marion. On digital and terrestrial.

Marion   I'd like to make a further statement.

A   Of course – please.

Marion   I'd like to say . . . Fuck the bastards. Fuck them. Fuck them. Round them up. Round them all up and take them up to the castle and tie them to a stake and burn them, burn them, burn them. Please, everyone at home – round them up and burn them.

Friend   I support you, Marion. I'm feeling what you're feeling and you're speaking for me.

Marion   Please help the authorities. Please put pressure on your elected representatives. Let none of us sleep till we've beaten down every last door and burnt every last piece of scum flesh.

One   Yes! Yes! Yes! Burn me!

A   Thank you, Marion. You see? You see, the eloquence of the ordinary man or woman when impelled to act is incredible.

C   Oh yes. Yes. We're all incredible, wonderful people, apart from the rotten eggs.

B   Look at the screens – there's news on the screens – news news news.

C   Turn up the sound.

Reporter (*TV acoustic, huge excitement in background*)   Oh yes! Yes! Yes! It's been passed. It's gone through on a fair majority. The bill has been passed. Our elected representatives say we can now brand people who witness the attacks and don't come forward. Fireworks and champagne. Champagne and fireworks.

The whole courtroom goes wild with excitement.

One   Oh, that is good news.

A   Oh my God, oh my God, oh my God.

One   That's marvellous. That is – oh yes! Hurrah hurrah hurrah! You three must punish me. Brand me!

A   I feel ill. Fear. Revulsion.

One   What does Marion say on the link? Get Marion on the link. Marion, are you there?

Marion (*hospital acoustic*)   That is fan-fucking-tastic. That is . . . Democracy and truth democracy and truth democracy and truth democracy and truth democracy and truth democracy and truth democracy and truth. We can brand the rotten eggs!

Crowd (*at hospital*)   Democracy and truth.

Marion   Fireworks and champagne.

Crowd   Champagne and fireworks.

In the distance we can hear bells ringing, cheering, fireworks.

A   Did we come to power to carry through this awful burden of branding?

One   Please. Let me speak. People of this great city – the people of this great city of trade and industry and commerce – we are celebrating. We are celebrating that a wise decision has been made. I am to be branded. My faith is restored . . . sometimes you think . . . you think . . . democracy is failing . . .

You think . . . I don't know . . . it's not working . . . why this
vote, this cross on this box? Why? Sometimes you can't . . .
until something comes along, something, and hope is, trust and
hope and – God bless democracy – hope and trust are reborn.
Give me some some champagne, hurrah hurrah hurrah!

Pause.

Who will brand me? You?

A   . . . I can't.

One   You?

B   . . . I can't.

One   You . . . ? Please . . . Justice must be done.

C   Alright. I'll do it.

One   You can now brand anyone who witnessed yesterday's
incident but does not come forward. Under medical and legal
supervision, an iron heated to an exact temperature of 250
degrees centigrade will be applied to the right arm just here
until a permanent mark is left. Do you understand what you
must do?

C   I understand.

One   Heat the iron. I'm ready. Begin my punishment.

C   I'm starting to heat the iron.

An initial sizzle.

B   Stop, stop. We're getting a . . . There have been some
amendments.

A   Oh. The liberals. Thank God. The plasma screens.

Unease in the courtroom.

Reporter   Some amendments were made during the passing
of the bill in the interests of a humane society.

A   As we surely are.

Reporter   The branding will take place only in courtrooms
such as this one. TV crews and commercial radio stations will

have to bid for a franchise to broadcast. And calls for burning at the stake at the castle have been, as they say, 'kicked into the long grass'.

One   Not as harsh as I hoped but . . . Oh well, still . . . a victory for democracy and humanity. Oh . . . Yes yes. Democracy and humanity. Democracy and humanity. Our core values. Once again they shine through in every act of our enlightened society. Please, is the iron heated?

C   The iron is being heated.

One   Let the iron be heated faster.

A   But . . . You understand? Branding will hurt. We won't pretend –

One   Oh yes. I will be a pariah for – ooh – decades.

B   But listen, listen, there'll be forgiveness. Somewhere. There's always kind, liberal, kind, forgiving, liberal, kind people who will forgive. There's always refuge from the mob. There's kindness in the world. There's always liberals.

One   I don't want the liberals. Horrible.

A   Your branding will be humane. So different from our enemies. In our enemies' countries, people are dragged kicking and screaming into public places and they are branded without proper medical or legal supervision. Revolting. My stomach is turning. Turning. There – in the heart of that evil empire – people are burnt frequently at the stake. Ugh. Ugh. Their only crime? Their only crime? What is their only crime? Their only crime – It's . . . Oh yes.

C   The iron is nearly hot enough.

A   Their only crime – thank you – their only crime is to stand up and say: 'I am a person. I am my own distinct person. I have my own personality and my own thoughts.' And for this, these people are burnt. Disgusting. Disgusting. Disgusting. How they yearn for freedom and light and choice, democratic choice, for rights and responsibilities. How they yearn and how we, many of them, take them for granted.

B   The iron has now reached 250 degrees.

C   Bring the guilty one forward for punishment.

One   I come forward and thank this audience, the city, the listeners, the nation for my punishment.

Footsteps as he is brought forward.

A historical moment. This is history. I am the first person – correction – the first rotten egg to be branded since the passing of the new legislation. It is happening in front of the audience here and at home.

C   Do you have words, do you have things that you would like to say to that audience?

One   I do.

C   Well, my friend, now is your moment, now is the moment, now is your time, so . . . speak.

One   I . . . I am a rotten egg. I know that now. The mark will be here on my arm for all of you to see. Like a broken wing. Please despise me, please hate me, please brand me. That is your right – and your responsibility. I will be forever recognisable to the rest of you. You go to a beach or a cocktail party or a – You sit out there in the shopping centre drinking your coffee and eating your pastry and I will be recognisable to the rest of you. There he goes – there he goes, the scumming, cancer, rotten dregs, the stinking out the barrel the . . . How I wish I could lead a normal life. Paint watercolours. Go fly fishing. Teach my daughter Spanish. Talk online with my friend in Southern Australia. But this will never happen. I am evil and I have been banished from Paradise forever. This is justice and I embrace it. I did not come forward. I witnessed a violent incident in the shopping centre and yet I did not come forward. Why didn't I . . . ? For one reason and one reason alone. I am a bad person. There is no point trying to understand me. There is no point giving me money. I am bad bad bad bad bad. Please assist the authorities. Please report violent incidents. Please come forward.

I would like 'Fireworks' by Handel for my branding.

A   Oh yes. Handel. There should be Handel for the branding. Let there be Handel. Offer your arm for the branding.

One   I offer my arm for the branding.

A   Now. Now. Handel, speak for us. Handel, give us thy spirit as we celebrate this moment of history. Let us celebrate this branding.

Handel plays on disc, swelling.

One   Hurrah for the normal!

Crowd   Hurrah for the normal, the normal, the normal!

One   Let the branding begin.

B   Let the branding begin.

A   Brand him.

The sizzle of the iron on flesh. **One** *screams.*

One   Agghhhh. God bless the – agghhh – cameras. God bless our elected – uuugh – representatives. Democracy and truth and history and freedom and . . . and . . . and . . . democracy and history and truth and – aaaaaghhhhhh!

The Handel ends.

A   Doctor, what's happened?

Doctor   He's lost consciousness – it's to be expected after a branding.

A   Then take him out. Remove the rotten egg.

Groans as **One** *is carried from the courtroom.*

A   Time for us all to go home. Back to your normal homes. Democracy has done its work. Justice has been done.

The courtroom starts to clear.

A (*to* **Usher**)   Democracy and humanity. Our core values.

B   Oh yes. Once again they shine through in every act of our enlightened society.

C   Do you know what I'm going to do now?

B   No. I don't know.

C   What I'm going to right now. Right now I'm going to have a great cup of coffee.

A   Ah yes. A great cup of coffee.

B   I think it's going to be a rather fabulous day.

C   Oh yes. For most of us it's going to be a fabulous day. But for the guilty ones there's always branding. (*Suddenly close to us.*) Are you a guilty one? Do you know a guilty one? You listening at home or in the car? Is there guilt?

B   We ask you this. Please help the authorities.

C   Please come forward. It's easy to make yourself known and to be identified in a multimedia democratic broadcasting environment. It's important if we are to end these troubled times. That we end these series of unprovoked attacks.

A   End them. And let freedom and democracy and justice shine forth across the globe. Forever and evermore.

A/B/C   Hurrah hurrah hurrah!

A   Goodnight.